To Dad

With Lots of Love

From

Kevin x & Maria x

Phantom – From The Cockpit

PHANTOM – FROM THE COCKPIT

Peter Caygill

Pen & Sword
AVIATION

First published in Great Britain in 2005 by
Pen & Sword Aviation
an imprint of
Pen & Sword Books Ltd
47 Church Street
Barnsley
South Yorkshire
S70 2AS

ISBN 1 84415 225 1

A CIP catalogue record for this book is available from the British Library.

Typeset in 10/12 Times New Roman by
Concept, Huddersfield, West Yorkshire

Printed and bound in England by
CIP UK

Pen & Sword Books Ltd incorporates the Imprints of Pen & Sword Aviation, Pen & Sword Maritime, Pen & Sword Military, Wharncliffe Local History, Pen & Sword Select, Pen & Sword Military Classics and Leo Cooper.

For a complete list of Pen & Sword titles please contact
PEN & SWORD BOOKS LIMITED
47 Church Street, Barnsley, South Yorkshire, S70 2AS, England
E-mail: enquiries@pen-and-sword.co.uk
Website: www.pen-and-sword.co.uk

Contents

	Acknowledgements	vii
	Introduction	ix
1	Design and Development	1
2	Deck-Landing Trials	9
3	F-4K Intensive Flying Trials	18
4	Spey Development and Early Service Problems	26
5	First Impressions	34
6	The Phantom At Sea – An Artificer's View	42
7	Phantom Tactics – Penetration	54
8	Phantom Tactics – Air Defence	63
9	F-4J Handling Characteristics	74
10	Accidents and Incidents	88
11	Crew Debrief – 1	102
12	Crew Debrief – 2	119
13	Phantom Test Pilot	132
14	Phantom Flight	141
	Glossary	154
	Appendix 1 – Phantom FGR.2 Performance and Speed Limitations	157
	Appendix 2 – Phantom FGR.2 Selected Emergency Procedures	160
	Index	171

Acknowledgements

The inspiration for this book came from Wing Commander Peter Desmond, a highly experienced night-fighter navigator whose long RAF flying career included testing the Phantom at A&AEE, Boscombe Down, and completing tours at Bruggen in 2ATAF and at Leuchars with 43 Squadron. Peter had already helped me with a previous book on the early RAF jet fighters, and suggested doing something similar, but dealing solely with the Phantom. As an incentive he furnished me with the relevant sections of his unpublished autobiography which provide a fascinating insight into what it was like to be a member of the Phantom force in the early 1970s.

Along the way I have had considerable help from others who were associated with the Phantom in various capacities. I would especially like to thank Don Headley for his help and hospitality. After a career in the RAF, Don had a brief spell as a ferry pilot before becoming a test pilot with Hawker Siddeley (later BAe), eventually taking over as Chief Test Pilot at Holme-on-Spalding Moor with responsibility for the Phantom and Buccaneer. I was also very fortunate to be put in touch with Group Captain Mike Shaw CBE who had a long career on Phantoms commencing in 1964 when he became one of the first RAF exchange pilots to fly the F-4 with the US Marine Corps. In the mid-1970s he commanded 228 OCU at Coningsby and has almost 1,400 hours on type.

I am also deeply indebted to Lionel Smith who was an artificer on HMS *Ark Royal* in the early days of the Fleet Air Arm's involvement with the Phantom. Maintaining a complex fighter aircraft is difficult enough at the best of times, but in the cramped confines of an aircraft carrier the task is invariably made much more difficult. Lionel's descriptions of the conditions he had to work in make for compelling reading. My special thanks also go to Bob Cossey of the 74 'Tiger' Squadron Association for allowing me to include an account of his flight in an F-4J; to Group Captain Chris Sprent, former O.C. 31 Squadron; and to Guy Woods who spent ten years as a navigator on Phantoms in a career that saw him involved with every RAF night/all-weather fighter from the Meteor NF.12/14 to the Tornado F.3.

I would also like to thank Group Captain Graham Clarke for his recollections of flying the Phantom with 92 and 74 Squadrons and for kindly allowing me to borrow various items of Phantom-related material; Wing Commander Anthony 'Bugs' Bendell OBE AFC for allowing me to quote from his autobiography 'Never In Anger', and Philip Jarrett for helping out once again with photographs.

Much research was also carried out at the National Archives at Kew and I would like to thank the staff for their help in locating the various documents relating to the Phantom in RAF and Royal Navy service.

Introduction

The McDonnell Douglas F-4 Phantom has gone down in history as one of the most important multi-role fighter aircraft ever produced. It provided the backbone of US operations in Vietnam and was equally at home carrying out strike operations from aircraft carriers or providing top cover to ward off attacks by MiG-21s. It was flown by numerous air forces throughout the world, and saw action with the Israeli Air Force during the Yom Kippur War in 1973, and with Iran during the conflict with Iraq. When the production lines at St Louis eventually fell silent a total of 5,057 examples of the F-4 had been produced.

The Phantom was flown by the Royal Navy and RAF in somewhat unfortunate circumstances following the cancellation of the Hawker P.1154, but it was to provide a quantum leap in capability and was loved by all who flew it. The British Phantom was, however, much different from its American counterpart. The airframe was re-engineered to accept Rolls-Royce Spey engines which provided vital work for the British aviation industry, but resulted in an aircraft that was much more expensive and lacking in performance in several respects. As one Phantom navigator put it, 'if you want a brief on how to screw up a fine aeroplane, read the UK Phantom history!'

This book looks at the British version of the Phantom from the point of view of the crews tasked with flying it. Performance and handling characteristics, together with the results of pre-service trials, are interspersed with numerous first-hand accounts of pilots and navigators. The tactics adopted by the RAF for penetration/strike missions and for air defence are included, as are some of the incidents that befell Phantom crews when things did not go according to plan. The difficulty of operating high performance aircraft on an aircraft carrier are graphically illustrated by an account of life aboard HMS *Ark Royal.*

During the twenty-four years that it was in service with the RAF/RN the Phantom came to be regarded with great affection, even by those pilots who converted to it from the English Electric Lightning. Although the latter aircraft possessed better handling qualities, the Phantom's greater endurance, extensive weapons load and much superior radar meant that most former Lightning jocks preferred the F-4 overall, even if it meant putting up with the 'talking baggage' in the back seat! Although phased out by the RAF in 1992, the Phantom is still in widespread service with air forces throughout the world and looks set to continue flying long after the fiftieth anniversary of its first flight in 2008.

CHAPTER ONE

Design and Development

At the time of its first flight in May 1958 the McDonnell Douglas F4H-1 Phantom II represented a radical departure from what had gone before, with respect to both design and concept. The first decade of jet-powered flight had seen dramatic progress in the performance levels of fighter aircraft, especially in terms of climb rate and top speed and it is, perhaps, not surprising that most aircraft of the 1950s had a relatively short life in their primary role as they were quickly supplanted by more advanced machines. Many aircraft had also experienced a troubled development, particularly in relation to handling problems encountered in the transonic region of flight, but these difficulties were gradually being overcome. The first experience of jet versus jet combat over Korea also led to changed thinking as regards the type of aircraft that were needed and the tactics to be employed. The Phantom was very much a product of the Korean War and with the benefit of hindsight it would be easy to suggest that the F4H was a star awaiting a stage, however, at the time of its inception there were still many doubts and uncertainties, and very few people at the time could have envisaged how important a design it would be, or how long its eventual pre-eminence would last.

By the mid-1950s McDonnell had already produced three jet fighters for the US Navy. The straight-winged XFD-1 (later FH-1) Phantom was the world's first purpose-built naval jet fighter and was powered by two Westinghouse J30 turbojet engines, each producing a modest 1,600 lb s.t. With a top speed only approaching 500 mph the first Phantom had little operational capability and only sixty were produced. The FH-1 was followed by the F2H Banshee which was broadly similar in design but was powered by two Westinghouse J34s rated at 3,000 lb s.t. The type saw widespread use in the Korean War and was developed with a stretched fuselage to allow more internal fuel to be carried, culminating in the

F2H-4. It was also produced in night-fighter and photo-reconnaissance versions. The next version produced by McDonnell was the single-seat, swept-wing F3H Demon which was initially powered by the troublesome Westinghouse J40 of 7,200 lb s.t., and later, in the F3H-2 version, by the Allison J71 rated at 14,250 lb s.t. with reheat. The F3H-2 Demon was used as a carrier-based all-weather fighter and remained in service until August 1964.

With experience gained from producing the Banshee and Demon, and with war still raging in Korea, McDonnell began to look to the next generation of naval fighter and in 1953 took a proposal to the Bureau of Aeronautics at the US Navy. Known at first as the F3H-G, McDonnell's design philosophy embraced a multi-role capability for the new aircraft which manifested itself in a series of seven different nose sections which could be interchanged to suit each individual role. These included interceptor, attack, photographic reconnaissance and electronic countermeasure (ECM) roles. From the outset it was established that the new aircraft would have to be powered by two engines, but at this early stage in its evolution it was still very much a single-seat design. Weight was likely to be significantly greater than the previous generation of naval fighters, the initial estimate of 45,000 lb being approximately 50 per cent greater than the all-up weight of the F3H.

The proposal from McDonnell was formulated at a time of considerable change in military aviation. Technological advances in aircraft structures and improved engine performance held the prospect of dramatic improvements in performance capability. At the same time the doctrine of air combat was coming in for close scrutiny following the war in Korea. Conflicts between USAF F-86 Sabres and MiG-15s flown by Communist forces during this particular conflict appeared to show that the day of the gun was over and that the air-to-air missile (AAM) would be the weapon of the future. This led to an instruction being passed to McDonnell from the Bureau of Aeronautics to delete the four 20 mm Colt cannon installation that had originally been proposed and replace it with four Sparrow AAMs as the aircraft's sole offensive capability in the interceptor role. Several other Services around the world came to the same unfortunate conclusion. However, American experience during the Vietnam War demonstrated that aerial dogfights were not a thing of the past, and that the gun was still a useful weapon to have on board.

With the trend towards much larger aircraft carriers, as typified by the 76,000 ton Forrestal-class carriers that were under construction as the Korean War was coming to a close, McDonnell were able to take advantage of the improved facilities, particularly in relation to deck length, to create an aircraft that was larger, heavier and much more powerful than anything that had gone before. The fact that an aircraft of much greater performance and capability was needed was confirmed by Intelligence reports coming out of the Soviet Union that suggested the aviation industry there was making rapid strides in fighter design. The Mach 1.5 capable MiG-19 had been flown in prototype form in April 1952, with production orders being placed two years later, and this aircraft was rapidly followed by early versions of the ubiquitous MiG-21, which was to be produced in greater numbers than any other jet fighter. It was now abundantly clear that Soviet fighter designers were more than capable of developing state-of-the-art aircraft, a realisation which came as something of a shock to the Western democracies which had tended to downplay the ability of the Eastern Bloc to produce advanced aircraft. With this spur, McDonnell set about formulating what would become the most important warplane in the West.

The first wooden mock-up produced in early 1954 showed a distinct resemblance to the F3H Demon in overall configuration, with a low mounted swept-wing mated to a fuselage incorporating side-mounted engine intakes. The only major variation was the adoption of a twin-engined layout, the exhaust being located under the rear fuselage. At this stage the aircraft had a conventional tailplane and the wing exhibited only slight dihedral, although this was soon to be changed to one with marked anhedral to avoid disturbance from the wing at high angles of attack and to ease problems with pitch-up which was afflicting many other swept wing aircraft of the period. The engine initially chosen for the F3H-G was the Wright J65 turbojet (licence built Sapphire) which was rated at 8,000 lb s.t., but this was quickly replaced by the new General Electric J79-GE-2 which was expected to produce around 15,000 lb s.t. with reheat.

Between the first and second mock up stages the decision was made to delete the gun armament in favour of air-to-air missiles and McDonnell's proposal to supply interchangeable nose sections to cater for the aircraft's differing roles came under close scrutiny. Eventually it was decided to do away with this facility and make the new machine a two-seater for all the missions it was to undertake. At the same time the attack role was removed from the requirement and this mission was later carried out by the North American A-5 Vigilante. As befitting its multi-role capability, eleven external store positions were incorporated, comprising five under each wing with one under the fuselage centreline.

At a fairly late stage in the design evolution of the F4H the outer wings were given 12 degrees of dihedral to improve lateral stability, and at the same time the chord was increased on the outer section so that a 'dogtooth' occurred at the point of wing crank which had the effect of creating a marked vortex. This was an attempt to reduce the spanwise flow of air to delay tip stalling, a major factor in pitch-up. The decision to use the J79 engine meant that considerable re-profiling of the intakes was needed to cater for the increased mass flow of the new engine. The necessity to deliver the correct amount of air for any flight condition over a wide speed range resulted in a highly complex duct design in order to produce the appropriate shock wave so that air entering the engines was always travelling at subsonic speeds, even when the aircraft was flying at speeds approaching Mach 2.0.

A wide track undercarriage was provided to endow good deck landing characteristics, the gear itself being able to cope with a rate of descent of 22 ft/sec. The control surfaces comprised ailerons mounted on the inner portions of each wing which operated together with a spoiler on the opposite wing to provide lateral control. Movement in pitch was by the 'slab' tailplane and a normal rudder was fitted to provide directional control. With landing speeds tending to increase with every advance in overall performance, it was especially important to explore ways of slowing the approach speed of the new breed of naval fighters. This was achieved in the F4H by utilising high pressure air from the aircraft's engines to blow over the leading and trailing edge flaps to re-energise the boundary layer to prevent a breakdown of airflow at high angles of attack.

The change from single to two-seat configuration had resulted in a revision of the amount of internal fuel to be carried and the capacity was eventually settled at 1,665 Imp gallons in six fuselage-mounted tanks. In addition a 500 Imp gallon overload tank could be carried on the fuselage centreline together with two tanks under the wings, each of 308 Imp gallons. A retractable flight refuelling probe was also located on the right-hand side of the cockpit. The prototype F4H-1 (BuAer No. 142259) was flown for the first time on 27 May 1958 by McDonnell Chief Test Pilot Robert C. Little from Lambert Field, St Louis. Little took the F4H-1 to a speed of Mach 1.68 on only its third flight and testing continued thereafter at Edwards Air Force Base, California.

The original 24 in scanner of the Westinghouse AN/APQ-72 radar was replaced by one of 32 in diameter to provide increased range performance, an enlarged and lowered nose being required to accommodate the new dish. At the same time the nose profile was further changed by the addition of a secondary radome for the AAA-4 infra-red seeker. The opportunity was also taken to raise the rear cockpit and modify the canopy to create more space and improve the Radar Intercept Officer's lookout. Further modifications had to be made to the air intakes with the introduction of J79-GE-8 engines of increased performance, each offering 17,000 lb s.t. with reheat. To avoid confusion, all previous aircraft powered by J79-GE-2 engines were henceforth referred to as the F4H-1F, with subsequent machines fitted with the -8 engine being known as the F4H-1. Because it was showing every sign of being an extraordinary creation, McDonnell decided to make the F4H the centrepiece for its twentieth anniversary celebrations which were to take place in July 1959. In a special ceremony at St Louis the F4H was officially named Phantom II, the same name as that used for the company's very first jet fighter.

Manufacturer's and US Navy trials continued to proceed satisfactorily and culminated in the Board of Inspection and Survey (BIS) trials which were commenced at the experimental establishment at Patuxent River in July 1960. During the next five months the Phantom surpassed all expectations and exceeded all its operational requirements by a large margin. Such was the level of confidence that was beginning to build around the aircraft that McDonnell proposed to use the Phantom for an all-out attack on a whole series of World Records. Eventually, the Phantom became the holder of the records for absolute speed at low and high levels, in addition to those for altitude and sustained altitude. Project *Sageburner* resulted in a speed of 902.769 mph (Mach 1.25) being set at low level over the White Sands Missile Range in New Mexico on 28 August 1961, with Project *Skyburner* raising the high-level speed record by no less than 43 per cent to 1,606.51 mph (Mach 2.59) later the same year. The altitude record (Project *Top Flight*) had already been successfully claimed on 6 December 1959, with a figure of 98,557 ft being achieved following an energy climb.

The aircraft used for *Top Flight* was the second prototype BuAer No. 142260 flown by Commander Laurence E. Flint Jr, USN. In preparation for the record attempt as much equipment as possible was removed, including the radar. Fuel flow and maximum engine rpm were also increased, together with modifications to the nozzles to increase power in reheat. The flight was carried out from Edwards Air Force Base and involved a climb to 50,000 ft followed by acceleration to Mach 2.38 before the Phantom was put into a near vertical climb. The ascent followed a ballistic trajectory whereby Flint was weightless as the nose of the aircraft was gradually lowered so as to obtain maximum performance. The engines flamed out in the rarefied air and the pilot maintained forward stick, topping out just below the magic figure of 100,000 ft. The initial part of the descent required fine handling as speed had fallen well below the normal stalling speed, but with a return to denser air the engines could be relit and Flint landed back at Edwards after a flight lasting 40 minutes (this record only stood for eight days before a new record was set by an F-104C Starfighter flown by Captain J. B. Jordan on 14 September 1959 with an altitude of 103,389 ft). Other records were set by the Phantom including that for sustained altitude with 66,443 ft being recorded on 5 December 1961. A number of time-to-height records were also claimed.

The Phantom entered service with the US Navy on 29 December 1960 when F4H-1 148256 was taken on charge by VF-101 at Miramar in California. The first operational deployment occurred in August 1962 when VF-74 flew from the USS *Forrestal* which was sailing in the Mediterranean. The US Marine Corps began to take delivery of the F4H-1 Phantom in June 1962 although this designation was soon changed to F-4B under a revised classification introduced in September 1962. Around this time the Phantom was also taken on by the USAF which was in need of an aircraft to fill the gap between the 'Century-series' of fighters developed in the 1950s and the swing-wing TFX project (F-111) which was still some way from entering service. The F-4C for the USAF featured J79-GE-15 engines which were equipped with cartridge start as opposed to the externally assisted air start of Navy Phantoms. The flight refuelling probe was deleted in favour of a standard orifice to accept the Air Force's 'flying boom' system as used by KC-135 tankers, and the wheels and tyres were enlarged to keep temperatures within limits during operations from tarmac runways. In Air Force service the back-seater was known as a Weapon System Operator (WSO) and the radar used was the AN/APQ-100. The first F-4C for the USAF made its maiden flight on 27 May 1963 and the type became operational with the 12th Tactical Fighter Wing at McDill Air Force Base (AFB).

The Phantom was soon attracting attention from abroad, with the Fleet Air Arm at the head of the queue. Throughout the early 1960s Hawker Siddeley had been developing the vertical take-off P.1154 as a supersonic fighter for both the RAF and the Royal Navy, but as time passed it became clear that the conflicting requirements of the two services were causing irreparable damage to the whole programme. The RAF was looking to the aircraft to provide single-seat ground attack, whereas the FAA wanted a two-seat, high-level interceptor. The crunch came towards the end of 1963 when the decision was taken to continue with the development of the P.1154 in a form which favoured the RAF version. This effectively killed the Naval variant which, paradoxically, played into the hands of the Admiralty because they had wanted the Phantom all along (with one of its two customers gone, however, the P.1154 was severely weakened and the project was cancelled completely by the Labour Government that came to power in October 1964).

McDonnell had been actively courting the Fleet Air Arm for some time and had already looked into ways of making the Phantom compatible with British aircraft carriers. The Royal Navy had always questioned the suitability of the Bristol Siddeley BS.100 engine intended for the P.1154 and the Admiralty preferred the Rolls-Royce Spey that was already powering the Buccaneer low-level strike aircraft. By the time that the official announcement was made on 27 February 1964 that the Naval version of the P.1154 was dead and that the service would be receiving an Anglicised Phantom instead, feasibility studies were already well in hand.

The British Phantom was based on the F-4J which had been flown for the first time on 4 June 1965. The J79-GE-10 engines as fitted to the 'J' were replaced by the Spey turbofan which offered around 20,000 lb s.t. with reheat. Although significantly more powerful, the Spey had a larger diameter than the J79 which meant that the centre section of the aircraft had to be redesigned to accommodate it. The air intakes also had to be enlarged by 20 per cent to cope with the Spey's increased mass flow. The net result was that the top speed performance was actually reduced by a considerable margin: the British Phantom only managing Mach 1.9, whereas the F-4J was limited to Mach 2.1. On the plus side take-off performance showed an improvement and fuel consumption was better. However, the decision to use the Spey was one that particularly appealed to the politicians because it also safeguarded jobs, although, it cost the taxpayer millions of pounds over and above the 'off the shelf' price; all for an aircraft that was actually less capable.

Designated F-4K, the Phantom for the Royal Navy also differed from its American counterpart in having an extendable nosewheel-leg to raise the angle of attack (AOA) in order to allow safe operation from Britain's smaller aircraft carriers. As the hangar lifts were also smaller, the nose radome had to be hinged so that it could swing through 180 degrees. The radar chosen was the pulse Doppler Westinghouse AN/AWG-10 licence built by Ferranti as the AN/AWG-11. Other features included larger flaps, drooping ailerons and slotted stabilators with slightly reduced anhedral. The first YF-4K (XT595) was flown at St Louis on 27 June 1966 and the type entered service with 700P Squadron at Yeovilton as the Phantom FG.1 on 30 April 1968.

In the meantime the RAF had also become a customer for the Phantom following the ultimate demise of the P.1154. The initial contract was placed in June 1965 and the aircraft was given the designation F-4M with the first aircraft (XT852) being taken on its maiden flight on 17 February 1967. The F-4M was similar to the Navy's F-4K except that many of the modifications to allow carrier operation were deleted. The F-4M thus featured a normal nosewheel leg and non-hinged radome, together with standard stabilators. Although it retained an arrester hook, the F-4M was not capable of carrier operation and was fitted with the Spey 202 engine which had a slightly slower reheat light-up than the F-4K's Spey 203. Unlike the F-4K, the RAF Phantom was capable of carrying the SUU-23 gun pod on the centreline attachment point. The first Phantom FGR.2 (XT891) entered service with the RAF on 23 August 1968 when it was delivered to 228 OCU at Coningsby and No. 6 Squadron became the first operational unit to convert in May 1969. Following the decision not to refit HMS *Eagle* for Phantom operations, twenty FG.1s originally intended for the FAA were transferred to the RAF, and were taken on by No. 43 Squadron which was re-formed at Leuchars on 1 September 1969.

CHAPTER TWO

Deck-Landing Trials

While the Phantom FG.1 was undergoing intensive flying trials in the UK, several deck-landing trials were conducted in the USA between 12 July and 1 August 1968. The trials were carried out by the Naval Air Test Centre, Patuxent River, using the USS *Coral Sea* which was sailing off San Francisco. The main trials aircraft was XT597, the first production machine, was configured to the latest production standard (i.e. Blue Plus standard engines with the latest throttle gearing) and featuring switching from twelfth to seventh stage compressor bleed as the throttles were advanced to full Military Power for increased thrust. It was also fitted with the automatic aileron droop retraction system (AADRS) that used a microswitch on the main undercarriage to initiate retraction of aileron droop as soon as the aircraft touched down; the aim being to assist in lifting the nosewheel quickly following a bolter. The third production Phantom FG.1 (XT859), was also used during the trial. It was also fitted with Blue Plus standard engines (but without the latest throttle gearing) and bleed switching, but, it did not have AADRS. Neither aircraft was fitted with an Automatic Power Control System (APCS) or any audio indication of Angle-of-Attack.

The main objectives of the trial were to demonstrate the catapult launch and to determine a suitable pilot technique and the minimum launch speed; the Specification figure for the latter being 129 kts True Air Speed (TAS) in full reheat at 44,600 lb and International Standard atmosphere (ISA) +25°C. Height loss during launch was not to exceed 6 feet. Approaches were to be carried out to demonstrate that the aircraft could be controlled on the glide slope and to assess any handling problems during overshoots and inadvertent bolters. The Boundary Layer Control (BLC) air offtake system was also to be evaluated. This system could be preset by the pilot to enable one, both or neither engines to switch to seventh stage bleed. The effectiveness of AADRS was to be assessed and it was also hoped to discover any deck compatibility problems that might exist. At this early stage no attempt was made to carry out any single engined approaches or night landings.

During the trials a total of twenty-two catapult launches were made, initially at the Specification weight of 44,600 lb using maximum reheat. The technique used at first was to hold full-back-stick (approximately −20 degrees tailplane angle) during the catapult stroke and then to ease the stick forward after launch to achieve 15–17 degrees nose-up attitude on the cockpit display. This method was adequate at the higher launch speeds (140 kts TAS) but at speeds close to the minimum this technique was soon discovered to be lacking. On the sixth launch at 122 kts TAS, full forward stick applied ¾ second after launch did not stop the aircraft over-rotating to 27 units AOA and experiencing a slight wing drop. Further launches were then made to investigate alternative methods using initial stick positions other than full back. The major difficulty with any revised technique was that the tailplane control circuit had little self centring and effectively no break out force and, therefore, it was virtually impossible to hold a given stick position, especially during the catapult stroke as the tailplane circuit was not balanced for the effects of longitudinal acceleration.

Pilot technique was obviously going to be the critical factor in defining an acceptable launch in the Phantom FG.1. Although full-back-stick on the catapult and pushing forward to a mid-position immediately after launch might be acceptable at reasonably high launch speeds and mid to forward Centre of Gravity (CG) positions, it was unlikely to be acceptable at lower speeds and aft CG. Because the difficulty of knowing quite where the stick was in anything other than the full back position, some form of 'stick position by feel' was highly desirable. As the trials progressed it also became obvious that the target attitude of 17 degrees nose up was too high and a more realistic figure would be 14–15 degrees.

Approaches made with full flap, aileron droop and 19 units AOA produced no outstanding problems in general aircraft handling, although there was still the general feeling that the Phantom was more difficult to handle in this condition than comparable aircraft. The major criticisms were poor thrust response leading to over-corrections in power setting, a general lack of stability and feel, rather heavy lateral control with quite a lot of break out force and a lack of rate information on the AOA display, the indexer 'traffic lights' not being adequate for this purpose. Approach speeds were generally in the region of 137 kts TAS at a weight of 36,000 lb and the bleed switching modification to the engines was highly commended as it provided a significant increase in thrust that was most welcome during overshoots. The associated nose-up pitching moment did not cause any problems. It was felt that if all aircraft were to be fitted with bleed switching, the AADRS modification would not be necessary as this system was only of benefit in helping to raise the nosewheel if bleed switching was inoperative.

Two of the recommendations to come out of the trial, namely 'stick position by feel' and an audio AOA to ease the pilot's task during the approach were evaluated during a further trial carried out by XT597 in October 1968 on the USS *J. F. Kennedy*. The main object of the stick positioning device used on the trial was to provide some indication of the workability of the general principle, and not necessarily to act as a trial installation of a system to go into production. Various devices were tested but all consisted of some form of connection between the stick head and the instrument panel. One scheme used nylon straps, one attached to the panel and one with a loop around the stick top, fastened together by means of Velcro pads which allowed an adjustment for length. If sufficient force was applied the pads would detach to allow full-back-stick to be reached in the case of an emergency.

Only four catapult launches were possible before the trial had to be prematurely terminated after a malfunction of the port engine. Despite this it was clear that the use of some form of stick positioning device was beneficial in that it resulted in launches that were more controllable and much more consistent. The pilot involved in the trial reported favourably on the device and it was found that the required tailplane angle could be held to an accuracy of around +/−1 degree. Simulated emergencies showed that if full-back-stick was required this could easily be achieved by applying a moderate stick force.

Details of the launches were as follows:

Launch	Weight	Catapult end speed	Wind over deck	Total	MLS
1	44,300 lb	121 kts	18 kts	139 kts	127 kts
2	45,100 lb	119 kts	17 kts	136 kts	131 kts
3	44,900 lb	107 kts	26 kts	133 kts	130 kts
4	44,800 lb	109 kts	22 kts	131 kts	130 kts

The Minimum Launch Speed (MLS) was calculated from a base figure of 125 knots in ISA conditions (15°C, 1013 mb), aircraft weight of 44,600 lb and full reheat. Corrections were then made for ambient temperature at the rate of +3 knots per +5°C, for ambient pressure at the rate of −1 knot per +10 mb and for aircraft weight at the rate of +3 knots per +1,000 lb.

A total of seven overshoots, seven rollers and five arrested landings were made during the trials, the primary aim being to assess the effect of the audio AOA fitted to the aircraft. The facility proved to be extremely useful and it noticeably eased workload in the pattern as well as on final approach, a benefit that was likely to be of even greater value when flying at night from British aircraft carriers. However, on the downside, it was noted that the poor engine and aircraft handling characteristics on the approach were still apparent.

Following the deck landing trials carried out in the US, a further brief trial was conducted in March 1969 on HMS *Eagle* to obtain more accurate figures in relation to approach and touchdown speeds. Clearance was given for a number of approaches and roller landings, but aircraft were not arrested during this trial. The two Phantoms used were XT857 and XT865, both of which were fitted with comprehensive instrumentation, but were aerodynamically to production standard. Both were modified so that the Boundary Layer Control (BLC) air offtake system was switched from twelfth stage to seventh stage compressor bleed when the throttles were advanced to the full Military Power (i.e. Non Reheat) stop. The audio indication of AOA was not fitted, however the standard dial presentation and indexer light system was installed. Due to their late arrival a third aircraft (XV567) was also used for a time, but this did not have the bleed switching modification.

The aircraft were flown along an approach path defined by a 4 degree setting on the Mirror Sight on the carrier. A nominal 19 units AOA was maintained by use of the AOA Indexer Light System which presented visual information of angle of attack. Whenever possible, if permitted by the ship pitch/aircraft weight limitations issued for the trial, the approach was continued to touchdown on the carrier for the subsequent roller. The standard technique was to apply full power at the point of touchdown, although on some occasions power was deliberately maintained at the approach setting until nearer the end of the angled deck, to simulate the case of an unpremeditated bolter and to assess any problems.

On the approach the mean speed recorded was approximately 138 kts EAS at an aircraft weight of 36,000 lb. However, the result of this trial and previous US experience showed that the calibrated airspeed (CAS) displayed to the pilot could differ from EAS by up to +/−4 knots depending on the aircraft being used at the time. General handling characteristics and control during approaches, wave-offs and bolters were considered just satisfactory for carrier operations, although poor longitudinal characteristics and slow engine response did increase the pilot's workload. Two points were considered unsatisfactory: the lack of sufficiently accurate information to obtain the correct approach speed and problems associated with the seventh to twelfth stage bleed switching. These and other aspects of the Phantom FG.1's landing performance are discussed in the following assessments which are based on the reports compiled by the pilots involved in the trials, Commander Hefford DSC and Lieutenant Commander Burn.

Approach

Finals Turn – A total of 119 approaches were made with the ship's projector light set to a 4 degree glide slope and wind over the deck of between 30–35 knots. The turn onto finals, in good weather, was commenced at approximately 600 feet at 155–165 knots with a power setting of 85–87 per cent, depending upon aircraft weight. Power was bled off in a slowly descending turn to arrive at the straight away on glide path with an 'on speed' indication and the approximate final approach power (82–84 per cent). The lack of longitudinal stick centring and feel required the pilot to pay close attention to AOA readings, up to 21.3 units (rudder pedal shaker) were occasionally seen when the pilot devoted too much attention to external references to adjust the turn, or was distracted by the need to confirm that bleed switch had not occurred. This lack of longitudinal stick centring and feel in the approach is unsatisfactory, but should just be acceptable for service use. Some compensation is likely to result when Audio AOA is fitted.

Line Up – Early in the trials a tendency to overshoot the centreline when rolling out of the finals turn was apparent. At this time the pilot's view of the ship changes from the left quarter windscreen panel to the front panel and due to distortion/parallax error a brief break occurs in visual reference. As experience was gained the centreline was overshot less frequently. Line up corrections were effected without difficulty at all stages of the approach, although if large lateral stick deflections were made the aircraft began to sink and the AOA reading increased. A combination of rudder and lateral stick was found to be the best technique, as it decreased the sink associated with aileron/spoiler-only corrections. Whilst the majority of rollers were made along the deck centreline, alignment errors were biased to the left resulting from insufficient pilot compensation for the axial wind component. The handling characteristics of the FG.1 are adequate to enable satisfactory line up during carrier approach and landing.

Glide Path – Glide path control was evaluated using constant attitude and varying power to make height corrections and as a separate technique, maintaining constant power and using a 'high dip' to correct for a high indication. Generally, correction for low indications was satisfactorily achieved with the addition of power while maintaining essentially constant attitude. However, the relatively slow thrust response of the Spey at approach power settings (82–84 per cent) resulted in a tendency to overcorrect. The best results were achieved by either making small power increases and allowing a slow correction to the glide path, or making a large transient power increase coupled with a small backward stick movement. Correction from a high indication with the use of power alone also resulted in a tendency to overcorrect. Use of the 'high dip' technique, or nose down nod at constant power gave good results. A controlled height correction could be made with only a transient excursion from datum conditions and without the need to change the power setting. A tendency to go high was observed when flying through funnel smoke and when entering airflow 'burble' close to the ship. As experience was gained this was controlled by a small forward stick movement. The handling characteristics of the FG.1 are adequate to give reasonable glide path control, but the thrust response characteristics complicate the pilot's task.

Speed Control – Evaluation of approach speed control was made firstly using the AOA index lights as a secondary reference with cross checks to the ASI, and secondly using a speed readout from the observer as primary reference with AOA index lights as a secondary reference. Small speed corrections were made with attitude control (fore-and-aft stick) while larger departures from datum required co-ordinated power and attitude adjustment. Using the index lights as primary reference, speed control on the approach was difficult. Cross reference to the ASI required a large eye movement and the small scale was difficult to read with a quick glance. Airspeed could change by as much as 4 knots with an 'on speed' indication before a fast or slow chevron appeared. Consequently, an acceleration or deceleration could build up before it was detected and a marked excursion from datum speed easily occurred. Rate of change of speed information is inadequate and approach speed control is unsatisfactory using this technique.

Using a speed readout from the observer as a primary reference, rate information was much improved. Additional reference to the index lights allowed correlation of attitude and airspeed changes and enabled datum speeds to be maintained within close limits (+/−2 knots). Use of audio AOA information as a primary reference may provide the required rate of information and its evaluation is recommended prior to the next deck trial. The approach speed control task using the observer to read out airspeed is satisfactory. The effect of airflow 'burble' at the round down on indicated airspeed changed with the ship's speed, natural wind speed and relative wind direction. Indicated airspeeds dropped between 2 and 5 knots without significant change of index light indication.

Forward Field of View – With the pilot's seat raised so that the pilot's helmet was just clear of the canopy, the forward field of view is entirely satisfactory at all stages of the approach and landing. Only one aircraft (XV587) was fitted with a pilot attack sight, but the reduction in field of view was insignificant.

BOLTERS

Thirteen simulated bolters were evaluated in XV587 without 'seventh at MIL' bleed switching and sixty-eight simulated bolters in the aircraft fitted with bleed switching. Military power and full-back-stick were normally applied on touchdown but slams to MIL power were delayed on a number of occasions, sometimes as late as the forward end of the angle. With 'seventh at MIL' bleed switching and slam to MIL at touchdown or soon after, no difficulty was experienced in raising the nosewheel before the deck edge and no handling problems were observed on leaving the ship, however, the forward CG limit case was not evaluated. Without bleed switching the nosewheel could not be raised and the aircraft left the ship in a flat attitude resulting in a slight sink or level fly away. The subsequent climb rate was noticeably slower with the reduced thrust in twelfth stage bleed.

When slams to MIL power (seventh at MIL) were made very late, the full-back-stick was held past the deck edge, the aircraft left the ship in a flat attitude and showed a marked tendency to over-rotate nose up as the stabilator entered free air (i.e. cleared ground effect) and as the nose-up trim change occurred with the switch to seventh at MIL. A large forward check of the stick was necessary to prevent rotation to high AOA readings. The maximum AOA indication obtained was 21 units, but due to the slow response of the servo controlled AOA system during high rates of pitch, the true AOA was probably significantly higher. An inclusion in Pilot's Notes is recommended to warn pilots of the possibility of over-rotation if the slam to seventh at MIL is delayed to the forward deck edge while holding full aft stick.

WAVE OFF

Wave off characteristics were evaluated with all three aircraft flown during thirty-eight overshoots at aircraft weights varying from 41,000–36,000 lb and with an average air temperature of approximately 8°C. No single engine wave offs were made. The additional thrust with 'seventh at MIL' switching was apparent in the improved performance, and for the conditions tested the wave off performance with bleed switching is entirely satisfactory. The nose up trim change on slamming to MIL with bleed switching was barely noticeable during the tests made and no objectionable handling characteristics were observed. For the test conditions the two engine wave off performance and handling characteristics of the FG.1 are satisfactory for service use.

BLEED SWITCHING

From the roller landings made, use of seventh at MIL bleed switching demonstrated improved bolter and wave off climb away performance and, for the test CGs, enabled nosewheel lift off to be made prior to reaching the forward deck edge. However, the control and indication of bleed switching was unsatisfactory. Bleed switching was initiated by forward movement of the throttles and occurred at a throttle position corresponding to rpms from 90 to 92 per cent. No bleed switch indication was installed in the cockpit. The low mean time between failure (MTBF) of non-return valves in the engine bleed system dictated that reversion from seventh stage bleed with full flap at MIL power to twelfth stage bleed should not occur. If seventh stage bleed was engaged with full flap extended, it was necessary to select HALF FLAP (thereby locking the bleed at seventh stage) before moving the throttles aft.

Average power settings downwind and on finals were 88–86 per cent and 84–82 per cent respectively, corresponding to 38,000–34,000 lb AUW [All-up Weight]. However, significantly higher rpms were required in correcting for airspeed and height excursions, particularly during the finals turn and straight away. The lack of longitudinal stick feel of the FG.1 resulted in frequent departures from the desired airspeed in the circuit, and subsequent large throttle movements. Also, correction for a low glide path indication required a large transient throttle movement. Both of the above conditions required the use of transient power increases up to and possibly exceeding the 90 to 92 per cent range with the subsequent risk of inadvertent bleed switching and valve damage. In hot weather higher power settings will be required and the risk of valve damage greatly increased.

The throttle-position bleed switching arrangement and lack of positive warning that bleed switch has occurred will lead to inadvertent and unrecorded operation of bleed switch in service, and is unacceptable with the low MTBF valves fitted at present. The need to raise the flaps to HALF before throttling back from MIL is a further embarrassment to the pilot. If the pilot observes an inadvertent switch to seventh he must select half flap before throttling back and may have to abandon the approach. Thus the control and indication of bleed switching with the present valves fitted are unsatisfactory for service use.

Chapter Three

F-4K Intensive Flying Trials

The first three Phantoms for the Royal Navy (XT858–860) were delivered to RNAS Yeovilton on 29 April 1968 and the following day No. 700P Squadron was commissioned in the presence of Flag Officer Naval Air Command, Vice-Admiral D. C. E. F. Gibson. Under Commander A. M. G. Pearson, the unit was tasked with carrying out intensive flying trials with the F-4K prior to the formation of two squadrons, one training (No. 767) and one operational (No. 892).

Although the Phantom had been in service with the US Navy since early 1961, the fundamental differences between the F-4K and the American version led to a number of problems arising during its introduction with the Fleet Air Arm. One of the main areas of difficulty lay with the Rolls-Royce Spey engine which suffered from a number of teething troubles, in particular, failures of the Constant Speed Drive Unit (CSDU). There were also several cases of engine over-temperature when airborne and it was felt that this problem was likely to be even more pronounced in service when the monitoring of turbine temperatures would not be as thorough as during the trials.

One such incident occurred on 2 September when a relight was attempted on the port engine of XT862 at 30,000 ft, Mach 0.65. The throttle was advanced to 90 per cent and after the Turbine Gas Temperature (TGT) had stabilised at 600°C, it then suddenly rose to 770°C which led the pilot to shut the engine down and make a rapid return to base. A check was made of the engine and it was declared serviceable for a check test flight after a period of ground running. On the test flight it was found that the engine stagnated on relighting at 30,000 ft at 27 per cent rpm and 300°C. The chase aircraft observed a considerable amount of smoke and haze coming from the port jet-pipe when the engine was in this condition.

The stagnation was eventually overcome by diving the aircraft to 27,000 ft.

Problems were also experienced with reheat light up and nozzle instability. On 6 September XT863 suffered a hard reheat light up on the port engine on take-off and a triple bang was heard, although it performed satisfactorily at all altitudes thereafter. On the same flight, when reheat was selected, the starboard nozzle appeared to be unstable and under and overshot its position three times before finally settling just below three-quarters open. At 0.95 M and 37,000 ft, the nozzle became unstable once again and pop stalling occurred with a drop in rpm of 5 per cent. When reheat was cancelled, the pop stalling cleared. Subsequent reheat light up was successfully accomplished by selecting the minimum setting and then waiting five seconds before advancing the throttles slowly to the maximum. In this case the nozzle appeared to be stable and the reheat performed well up to 1.55 M at 37,000 ft. Subsequent investigations during ground running revealed that the starboard engine pressure ratio ram had been incorrectly adjusted. Intake ramp vibration was experienced on XT864 but this was put down to a leak in the ramp hydraulic system. Of more concern were several cases of excessively high TGT when full flap was selected, further indication of potential trouble in the aft section of the Spey engine.

When first delivered the F-4K was fitted with an AN/ARN-86 Tacan which suffered loss of lock in the air-to-air mode whenever the aircraft was banked. A replacement Hoffman Tacan was first fitted in XT860 on 28 August and this proved to be entirely satisfactory in all operational modes. Problems were also experienced with the STR 70P radio altimeter which proved to be extremely unreliable with inconsistent readings. The best results were obtained when flying over the sea or over relatively flat or undulating terrain in straight and level flight, but even so, eight out of twenty-four checks showed grossly misleading or obviously inaccurate displays, either from the moment of switching the equipment on or at some stage in the trial.

Flights over hilly countryside, such as to be found at nearby Exmoor, and those involving rapid changes of altitude produced even worse results with six out of fourteen cases of unreliability. A major cause for concern was the tendency for the altimeter to indicate a random steady reading for some considerable time during a dive. In addition, records of spurious height indications when the aircraft was at very high level tended to add further conviction to the statement that the STR 70P was totally unreliable. Given its state of development at the time, the radio altimeter could only be regarded as a back up to the pressure altimeters pending the introduction of a more reliable system.

In addition to reporting on the Phantom's performance and determining its capabilities with regard to its varied roles, the trials unit also made an initial assessment of the best tactics to be used in the air defence role. For the interception of low level targets (250 ft AGL) it was considered that the firing of two Sparrow missiles in a forward quarter attack would be the ideal method. A locked-on pulse Doppler head-on attack was possible against a target at any speed, at any level, and the interception of very low level targets did not present any additional problems. However, difficulty in switching to pulse at low level precluded a positive lock-on every time and in a war situation could lead to a missed attack. Against subsonic targets this was not necessarily a total loss as the aircraft's excellent low level performance and radar operator capability could facilitate a delayed re-lock in pulse Doppler or pulse, or even a visual detection for a Sidewinder shot. When confronted with a supersonic target, however, this delayed re-lock usually resulted in a re-attack not being achieved.

A greater chance of success against fast, low level targets was possible if a pulse Doppler search attack into the rear hemisphere was planned. This was based on a typical Electronic Countermeasures (ECM) attack, using drift and bearing of the target. The pulse Doppler search presentation also provided an approximate target velocity and these factors, correctly interpreted, could provide an excellent chance of successfully achieving a Sidewinder kill. This technique did require a high degree of operator skill which could only be achieved through experience and constant practice.

Normal trials work was interrupted for a time in early September by participation in the Farnborough Air Show. The Royal Navy provided one of the most impressive displays ever seen at the venue comprising synchronised formation aerobatics by six Sea Vixens of 892 Squadron (Simon's Sircus) and five Buccaneers of 809 Squadron (Phoenix Five), together with a battle sequence featuring Wessex helicopters of 845 Squadron. Also in attendance were four Phantom FG.1s of 700P Squadron drawn from XT860–864, these being dubbed 'Pearson's Poppets'. Those who were there, including the author, will never forget the combined display, the finale of which saw all fifteen fast jets making low level passes at near sonic speeds before pulling up into vertical climbs. In addition, XT859 was used to demonstrate the superb low level performance of the Phantom in a solo routine and XT891, the first production aircraft for the RAF, was exhibited in the static display.

Shortly after appearing at Farnborough, XT859 was sidelined for a considerable period following failure of the rudder actuator. The actuator eye end had failed in fatigue and, although no obvious reason could be found at first, it was eventually considered that the most probable cause was excessive vibration during ground running at the sort of extreme engine conditions as would be required for a catapult take-off. This view was also shared by McDonnell Douglas as no problems of this nature had occurred on US Phantoms. All aircraft were grounded for one week but were allowed to fly again with a flight restriction of 4G in full reheat. Other aircraft having problems included XT863 which was out of commission for a number of weeks following a series of spurious fire warnings and XT869 which was grounded by an obscure generating defect. By this time it was becoming increasingly apparent to the F-4K maintainers that the standard of workmanship put into the Phantom by McDonnell Douglas left a lot to be desired. For a firm that, at the time, was well known for its posters publicising a 'zero defects drive', the result for the user was somewhat disappointing.

As the trial moved into the winter period, adverse weather conditions meant that most recoveries to Yeovilton were being made under actual instrument conditions and it was discovered that vertigo was experienced by a number of aircrew when flying under Instrument Meteorological Conditions (IMC) during Ground Controlled Approaches (GCA). This was attributed to the large change in attitude when speed was reduced from 250 knots, particularly during flap and aileron droop extension. The condition was aggravated when flying at night and in cloud by the flashing of the anti-collision light and other fuselage lights. It was concluded that the likelihood of crews suffering vertigo could be reduced if the aircraft was flown with the Automatic Flight Control System (AFCS) operational and if the anti-collision and white fuselage lights were switched off as soon as IMC conditions were entered. Even so it was a dangerous characteristic that had to be watched, particularly when training inexperienced aircrew.

In the early part of the trial the emphasis had been on determining aircraft and radar performance, followed by an evaluation of bombing using the ERU 119 ejector release unit which was capable of carrying three 540/1,000 lb bombs. Trials were also carried out with 2 in rocket projectiles (RP). Towards the end of the intensive flying period the majority of sorties involved Air Combat Manoeuvring (ACM). In order to obtain the optimum performance for manoeuvring it was essential that pilots had a clear understanding of the aircraft's aerodynamic characteristics. When subsonic below 420 Knots Calibrated Airspeed (KCAS) it was necessary to fly into heavy buffet to obtain the maximum turning performance. Until experience was gained, however, this could best be achieved by use of the Angle of Attack (AOA) gauge in the cockpit with 20 units AOA producing the maximum lift coefficient (CL) which provided the best instantaneous turn rate. Optimum sustained performance was obtained with a reading of 16 units AOA. For constant energy level turns, the onset of buffet was the criterion in this case, as angle of attack indication was of no value because it varied with speed, height and weight.

There were two areas in the flight envelope which were particularly sensitive and could lead to trouble if ignored. Adverse yaw induced by coarse use of aileron at high angles of attack could cause major embarrassment for a pilot in combat and, if it was necessary to maintain high AOA, it was best to manoeuvre by using the rudder. Longitudinal stability was also poor in the transonic region at high Indicated Airspeed (IAS) and a pilot induced oscillation (PIO) could easily be the result. If this happened, any inadvertent oscillation had to be countered by positive stick pressure. The operational effectiveness of the Phantom at specific altitudes depended to a large extent on the number of external stores being carried at the time, a situation that became apparent during level acceleration tests in the clean, medium and high drag configurations in military power. At medium drag the profiles flown confirmed that the Phantom was ineffective above 35,000 ft as there was virtually no additional energy available for turning, climbing or accelerating. In the high drag configuration the aircraft was operationally ineffective above 30,000 ft.

Although it possessed a formidable strike capability, the prime role of the Phantom FG.1 in Royal Navy service was air defence and as such it was most likely to come up against bomber/shadower aircraft of Tu-16 Badger, Tu-95 Bear or Tu-22 Blinder performance. In a non ECM environment these aircraft would have stood little chance against the Phantom weapons system, however, against very high targets, it was considered that maximum use would have to be made of the jump up capability of the Sparrow missile, since aircraft performance fell off rapidly above 40,000 ft. Low level shadowers could be detected on look down at a pulse Doppler radar range of sixty miles provided that they were closing with the fighter. If they were crossing, or the range was opening, the fighter had to descend to co-altitude for pulse radar pick-up and the maximum radar range would be reduced to twenty miles.

Combat Air Patrols (CAP) were fully evaluated at altitudes of 10–15,000 ft. To effect a successful interception, a low level target had to be picked up at a minimum range of 20 miles which was achieved by autonomous Phantom search or late warning from surface ships, although in an ideal situation Airborne Early Warning (AEW) from Gannet AEW.3s would significantly increase this figure. Depending on fighter weight, a high level subsonic threat could be attacked successfully from a CAP height of 12,000 ft given a minimum range of 30–40 miles and supersonic targets could be engaged at a range of 40–50 miles.

From a recommended CAP station at 12,000 ft and 100 miles from a carrier, the Phantom could extend the low level sensor warning range of the approach of hostile aircraft to the Fleet out to 150–180 miles, but it was stressed that this was an addition to, not a substitution for, AEW Gannet cover, a lesson that was forgotten with disastrous results during the Falklands War in 1982. Radar serviceability was the limiting factor on aircraft serviceability and at the time the intensive flying trials were being carried out by 700P Squadron, the mean time between failures (MTBF) of the radar was running at three hours. Based on a CAP cycle time of 1½ hours and assuming twelve aircraft in an operational squadron and the level of maintainer experience at the time, an MTBF figure of three hours was sufficient to keep one Phantom permanently on one CAP station. To keep two CAP stations operating an MTBF figure of 4½ hours would have been needed.

In the air defence role on CAP, as an escort fighter or engaged in fighter interdiction, if the Phantom was to be faced with opposing fighters they would most likely be of MiG-17 or MiG-21 performance. The Phantom FG.1 was markedly inferior to this type of aircraft in manoeuvrability and, therefore, its acceleration, climb and maximum speed performance, particularly at low level, had to be used in conjunction with the excellence of its weapons system to gain the advantage. This was to be achieved by employing slashing attacks, keeping the opponents at arms length and never mixing with them in close combat. During simulated air combat some problems were experienced with the Blue Plus standard Spey engines including over-temperature and flameouts during low airspeed vertical reversals at medium altitudes and above. The slow reheat lighting time was an operational penalty, and so also was the height restricted reheat lighting envelope which meant that pilots were reluctant to deselect reheat in a high altitude engagement. This resulted in extremely high fuel consumption rates of up to 1,000 lb/min.

Battle formation was fairly standard, although manoeuvring in formation had to be revised slightly because rear sector lookout in the Phantom was poor from both cockpits, with a blind area directly behind. In the strike role the Phantom could be loaded with up to 11,000 lb of bombs but it soon became apparent that when operating from a carrier, aircraft weight, Centre of Gravity and balance problems would limit the load. It was considered that a typical maximum load would be 10 × 540 lb bombs or four pods of 2 in Rocket Projectiles (RP) with no external fuel tanks. Realistic profiles gave a maximum strike radius of action of 300 miles or an endurance of twenty-five minutes in the target area when on close air support missions. The Phantom proved to be an extremely good weapons platform in dive attacks and the simple sighting method was well liked. Low level navigation presented no problems and good use could be made of the navigation computer and radar in the mapping mode. Provided there was no fighter opposition, radar was not essential for close air support and it was thought that the Phantom would be able to achieve a very high sortie rate in this role as radar serviceability was not an issue. In strikes over hostile territory, small numbers of Phantoms could achieve protection from ground fire by using high speed at very low level, but if maximum range was required the strikes would have to fly at high level, in which case some form of surface to air missile warning would be essential.

It was anticipated that the maximum all-up weight (AUW) of the Phantom for carrier launch would be in the order of 50,000 lb. This would allow for a centreline fuel tank to be carried together with four AIM-7E Sparrow and two AIM-9D Sidewinder missiles. Given a CAP station of 100 nm from the carrier, a launch/land cycle of 1 hour 45 minutes could be used comprising 30 minutes transit time and 1 hour 15 minutes loiter on station. This included a combat allowance for two high level supersonic interceptions and 2,000 lb fuel on return to the circuit.

The Phantom FG.1 did not possess the inherent characteristics of an air superiority fighter in the classic sense. Due to its relatively high wing loading and low thickness/chord ratio, sustained manoeuvring performance below 400 KCAS was poor. As with all heavy fighters, it suffered from high inertia levels which precluded rapid changes in direction. Above 25,000 ft excess thrust in Military Power was low which required almost constant use of reheat with attendant high fuel consumption. However, the high energy addition rates below 25,000 ft, good 'g' availability above 420 KCAS, good weapons system performance, excellent kill potential in the forward hemisphere and good minimum range capability of its air-to-air missiles, together provided enormous advantages for the FG.1. Providing certain fundamental principles were applied, coupled with its forward hemisphere kill potential, the Phantom was able to dictate the conditions of the fight and achieve a high degree of success in the Air Combat Manoeuvring (ACM) environment.

The following were considered to be the main operating procedures to be carried out when faced with fighters of MiG-17 and MiG-21 type.

a) Optimum cruise speed over enemy territory to be 400 KCAS/ 0.88 M.
b) Minimum engagement speeds at all altitudes – 450 KCAS.
c) Optimum manoeuvring speed/altitude – 450 KCAS/below 15,000 ft.
d) Never enter into close combat at altitude but either drag the fight down to below 20,000 ft or escape.

e) Execute a series of slashing attacks always maintaining a total energy advantage.

f) Do not allow the speed to decay below 350 KCAS unless coupled with considerable height advantage and then never below 250 KCAS.

g) Never allow the fight to degenerate into a turning match as all MiG aircraft have a greater 'g' availability and superior turn radius below 400 KCAS. Use the high energy addition rate capability below 15,000 ft and manoeuvre in the vertical plane.

It was found that by judicious use of reheat, average fuel consumption in an engagement at medium to low altitudes was around 450–500 lb/min, which was about half that used at high altitude as full reheat was constantly required.

The work of 700P Squadron was completed in early 1969. The unit was then disbanded and followed by No. 767 Squadron whose task was to train crews ready for the first (and last) operational Fleet Air Arm squadron, No. 892. Under Lieutenant Commander Peter Marshall, 767 Squadron also had the responsibility of training crews for No. 43 Squadron, the first RAF Phantom air defence unit, which was in the process of forming at Leuchars.

Chapter Four

Spey Development and Early Service Problems

The decision to adopt a reheated Spey engine in the British Phantom was largely based on the Royal Navy requirement for increased thrust over that of the standard J79 to allow safe operation from its smaller (than US) aircraft carriers, and also to increase significantly the input from British firms, still suffering after the swingeing defence cuts imposed by the Labour government in 1965. The reworked Spey soon ran into major problems however, and these were not to be fully overcome until the aircraft had been in service for some time.

The first US Navy Evaluation Trial on the F-4K took place in February/March 1967 and the subsequent report was critical of the Spey 201 in several aspects of its performance as follows:

a) Inadvertent throttle overshoots into reheat and idle cut off positions.

b) Inadequate throttle control so that it was impossible to set up a stable approach path for carrier operations.

c) Surging following slam accelerations into reheat.

d Inadequate reheat lighting and burning envelopes.

e) Inability to use maximum reheat due to excessive combustion roughness (buzz) such that the engine could not be operated at maximum reheat without the risk of mechanical failure of the reheat assembly.

f) Inadequate relight envelope.

g) Excessive idling rpm leading to high taxi speeds and brake overheating.

Following their assessment, the US Navy stated that they were not in a position to sanction production flight clearance or ferry clearance until the above deficiencies had been corrected. In response, Rolls-Royce designed a batch of modifications aimed at improving the Spey in the areas mentioned above, modified engines being referred to as Blue Standard engines, but even these were still below the full Spey 202 specification in several respects as follows:

a) Maximum thrust (full reheat) down by 8 per cent at 36,000 ft and Mach 1.1, and by 10 per cent at Mach 2.0.
b) Slam acceleration into reheat liable to result in failure to light if the slam was made from an initial power setting below about 50 per cent Military thrust.
c) Reheat light up ceiling about 17,000 ft below specification.
d) Reheat reliable burning ceiling about 5,000 ft below specification.
e) Engine relight ceiling limited to 25–30,000 ft when using AVCAT fuel.

The US Navy had also condemned the F-4K's suitability for carrier operations on two counts, excessive sink on wave-off, the aircraft taking six seconds to establish a positive rate of climb, and excessive ground roll before reaching rotation speed in the case of a bolter, the F-4K taking about 1,000 ft compared with 300 ft for the F-4J. The obvious need for more thrust to address these problems led Rolls-Royce to look towards reducing BLC bleed air flow, subject to flight tests by McDonnell Douglas to determine what reduction could be tolerated without increasing the minimum approach speed. Efforts were also made to reduce the acceleration time from approach power to Military power to 1½ seconds (from 2–3 seconds) and to achieve a reheat light up time of 1½ seconds (from 3 seconds). As the latter improvements fell outside the development contract, new funding was required and the Spey engine programme slipped by three months while the Blue Standard modifications were embodied.

By September 1967 the Spey was still deep in trouble having failed its 150 hour acceptance test due to HP1 turbine blade creep failure at 126 hours and to turbine blade cracking. Both were thought to be caused by burner carboning (by AVCAT fuel) which resulted in the engine running hot. As a result, doubt still existed as to whether the engine was reliable enough for safe transatlantic ferry, especially following a recent compressor stall incident with a production engine on the Rolls-Royce test beds. Development work led to a further set of modifications aimed, as far as possible, to bring the Spey's performance back to full specification. Engines so modified were designated Red Standard but the first examples were not expected to be ready for flight test until August 1968.

In the meantime the development programme continued and the initial CA release for the Phantom FG.1 for the Royal Navy was approved on 11 March 1968. The release contained a flight envelope which was less than that for an aircraft to full specification but which, nevertheless, contained no restriction on reheat handling at high altitudes and angles of attack. However, continued criticism in certain areas by Naval Air Test Center (NATC), Patuxent River led to further discussion before agreement could be given to the acceptance of production aircraft.

In all there had been fifteen cases of engine stalls and flame outs on one or other engine (on one occasion on both) following cancellation of reheat at altitudes between 32–45,000 ft, Mach Nos. 0.6–0.85 and at AOA from 12–22 units. As a result NATC recommended that a restriction be imposed on reheat operation to below 25,000 ft and less than 12 units AOA. Another concern was uncommanded thrust changes of significant size in the full flap approach configuration. It was hoped that this could be eradicated by adjusting the fuel control systems to a revised setting procedure. Not long after the Spey was hit by another problem when the Mark 202 began to suffer fatigue cracks in a rotating seal attached to the rear disc (twelfth stage) of the HP compressor. The Spey 201 engine as fitted to early F-4K aircraft was not affected. The immediate consequence was to halt the delivery of production engines while the situation was investigated, the Ministry of Technology subsequently decided that the flight life of the Spey 202 be restricted to 25 hours. Although this limitation was sufficient to cover production test flying at St Louis, it did not permit ferry operations over the Atlantic which meant that deliveries to the UK were suspended for the time being, except for those F-4Ks which were fitted with Spey 201 engines.

Despite the fact that the fatigue cracks in the rotating seal could occur very early in the engine's life, their rate of propagation thereafter was comparatively slow which gave hope that a flight life of 50 hours could be validated and this would, at least, allow ferry operations to be resumed. The ultimate aim was to extend the engine life to 100 hours, so that some worthwhile use of the aircraft could be made after delivery, and then to the original life of 150 hours by subsequent modification. Because of the continuing problems experienced with the Spey, aircraft delivery was, not surprisingly, badly hit and by mid 1968 deliveries were already twenty-three units behind schedule (eight F-4Ks and fifteen F-4Ms).

Following preliminary investigations, the manufacturers estimated that the revised Red Standard engine would have a maximum thrust which was fully up to specification at the performance guarantee point of 36,000 ft, Mach 2.0, but would be 5 per cent below the requirement at the same height at Mach 1.1. It was hoped that the reheat lighting ceiling would be improved, but no improvement was offered in the reheat combustion ceiling or in the AVCAT airstart envelope. Preliminary bench testing at Derby showed that maximum thrust was still some 1–2 per cent below specification and while some of the shortfall in the reheat lighting ceiling had been recovered, the reheat combustion ceiling had actually deteriorated. As production engines would not be available until early 1969, only the last few aircraft off the production line were fitted with Red Standard engines which meant that 380 engines needed to be modified by retrofit action.

Despite Rolls' best efforts, by March 1969 the expected performance from the Phantom fitted with Red Standard Spey engines still showed the following major shortcomings compared with the original requirement.

a) Maximum speed at altitude Mach 1.94 against Mach 2.1.
b) Supersonic/subsonic combat ceilings 51,700/48,600 ft against 54,700/51,500 ft.
c) Ferry range 1,680 nm against 2,170 nm.
d) LoLo strike radius of action 303 nm against 345 nm.
e) HiLoLoHi strike radius of action 484 nm against 670 nm.
f) CAP 1.45 hours against 1.90 hours.

From the operational point of view, the most serious deficiency was in the ceiling at which reheat could be operated. At a speed of Mach 0.90 these were expected to be 43,000 ft for lighting (as against the specification figure of 57,000 ft) and 51,000 ft for continued burning (as against 61,000 ft). These ceilings were considered to be inadequate, particularly in the Phantom's role as a fighter, even allowing for the effect of its weapons system.

Although the build up of the Phantom force significantly increased the capability of the Fleet Air Arm and the RAF, the Spey engine's development problems continued which meant that some difficult decisions had to be taken. The early 1970s was a particularly grim period for the RAF as the accident rate per flight hour of its principal interceptor, the English

Electric Lightning, showed a marked upward trend due to a worrying increase in the number of engine fires. In an eighteen month period commencing January 1970 no less than seventeen aircraft were lost, mainly as a result of in-flight fires or fire warnings, all this despite a Fire Integrity Programme that had been initiated in the late 1960s. The situation became so bad that, at one stage, it appeared that the future of the Lightning force was in doubt as numbers were dwindling at an alarming rate. Any continuation of loss rates on this scale would have seriously disrupted the RAF's planning, particularly because the Phantom was not due to take over air defence duties from the Lightning until the SEPECAT Jaguar had begun to enter service in 1974/5. Although Lightnings continued to be lost on a regular basis, statistics showed loss rates returning to more manageable levels and the type was to remain in service until finally withdrawn in April 1988.

At the same time as the Lightning was having its problems, the Phantom was also in serious trouble as a result of a sharp increase in the number of basic failures of the Spey 202 caused by HP1 turbine rotor blade failures at mid-height through thermal and mechanical stresses. This deficiency had been around from the very beginning and was one of the most serious to affect the Spey. As far back as January 1967 the F-4K Phantom Project Director, Captain K. R. Hickson, had reported as follows:

> Yet another engine has failed to complete the 150 hour type test which means that the flight life of the development engines cannot be extended beyond 75 hours. This is the third engine that has failed on type test. This short engine life, which was scheduled to be 150 hours by October last, considerably embarrasses the flight test programme, in which Rolls-Royce are already running some three months behind schedule on their deliveries. The present failure is of HP1 turbine blades and similar signs of failure have recently been found in a flight engine returned for overhaul. This is under current investigation but could mean that the present blade materials are unsuitable for the operating temperatures being used.

Development tests had already taken place on turbine blades modified to embody film-cooling which lowered blade temperature at the leading edges, thereby prolonging blade life. However, full implementation of this new process would inevitably take a considerable time, requiring the introduction of a number of palliative measures in an attempt to reduce the stress and temperature loadings of the HP1 blades. These measures included engine de-rating, operational limitations of engine handling techniques and the minimal use of the HP compressor twelfth stage bleed.

By late 1971 the Mean Time Between Rejection (MTBR) rate for the Spey engine was around 70 aircraft flying hours (140 engine hours) which was well below the figure that had been used to work out spare engine provisioning, as a Time Between Overhaul (TBO) of 400 hours had been assumed. When it came to overhauling engines the RAF had been experiencing problems with Rolls-Royce well before the Spey situation arose, in particular the length of time taken for these overhauls to be completed. Correspondence relating to this issue showed that several senior RAF officers were of the opinion that the upper management within Rolls-Royce at the time were pre-occupied with developing the RB.211 and other new civil transport engines rather than looking after existing business. Development difficulties with the RB.211 ultimately led to Rolls-Royce being placed in receivership in February 1971, but the company was born again three months later under new management whose attitude appeared to be rather more conducive to the needs of the RAF.

The situation within Rolls-Royce during this period was undoubtedly a factor in the problems afflicting the Spey but in the meantime it was up to the RAF to find ways of maintaining sufficient aircraft (and trained crews) to provide a credible deterrent. This was not easy as Rolls' were only able to supply, at best, twenty-seven overhauled engines per month which was well below the RAF's need to fulfil its flying task. By early 1972 all spare engines, including those in reserve aircraft, had been used and the aircraft on ground (AOG) rate had risen to 9 per cent.

Measures that could be taken to try to alleviate the problem included restricting maximum engine rpm, a reduction in the use of twelfth stage bleed during landing which had the effect of allowing the maximum cooling air to be applied to the turbine blades, and the education of air and ground crews in engine management. Deletion of the twelfth stage bleed was carried out by pulling the circuit breaker controlling the engine bleed valves. Unfortunately these same circuit breakers also controlled power supplied to the engine control amplifiers which, in turn, prevented over-temperaturing of the engines, the exact opposite of what was intended. This point was not appreciated by the staffs responsible for formulating the Special Flying Instruction (SFI) that was issued to those in the field and the proposal was initially cancelled. However, three months later, work by Rolls-Royce suggested that the degree of over-temperaturing was actually less than had originally been predicted and they proposed that the original SFI be reissued with an additional paragraph stating that where practice overshoots were planned the circuit breakers should remain 'unplugged'. Although there was the possibility of temperatures rising beyond limits in the case of an unplanned overshoot, it was felt that the effect of this on the number of engine rejections would be considerably more than offset by the deletion of twelfth stage bleed under normal landing conditions.

These revisions in operating procedures could not hope to address the problem fully and the only recourse was to reduce the number of flying hours of the Phantom fleet. Initial assessments were that the monthly flying task would have to be reduced by 20–25 per cent given the prospect of no immediate increase in the number of overhauled engines being returned from Rolls-Royce. Figures such as these equated to around 5–600 flying hours per month which was likely to have far reaching effects, both on the efficiency of the frontline squadrons and the training commitment at 228 OCU. It also held the prospect that trained crews from the OCU would be posted to an operational squadron where no flying would be available to them.

By early December 1971 Air Vice Marshal D. G. Evans, ACAS (Ops), was reporting that an extremely serious situation had arisen in the Phantom fleet due to the 'totally unforeseen' failure rates of HP1 turbine blades. Total engine 'holes' in aircraft amounted to thirty-six of which twenty-four were in front line aircraft and the AOG rate as a whole represented 10 per cent of the force. Superimposed on this acute short term problem was one of a general shortage of aircraft due to various essential engineering programmes, i.e. major servicing, fatigue programme, surface finish, radar update, INAS (Inertial Navigation and Attack system) retrofit, modification backlog, the fitment of Instrument Landing System (ILS) and a passive warning radar. As a result of these measures alone the RAF were faced with a deficiency in the planned front line strength of between 7–16 aircraft from 1972–76. As the RAF's priority was to carry out in full its obligations to Supreme Allied Command in Europe (SACEUR) in RAF Germany, the only room for manoeuvre in terms of the total number of Phantom hours flown were those in the 38 Group, Air Support Command squadrons and at 228 OCU. Any cutback in OCU throughput was likely to have serious implications in terms of planned aircrew/aircraft ratios and would probably place the future manning of the Jaguar force in jeopardy, but there was little choice if current commitments were to be maintained. The situation was further underlined by Air Marshal Sir Harold Martin, CinC RAF Germany, who reported that Phantom unserviceability was becoming critical and the current total of nine engine 'holes' in his force was only one away from the point at which training would be seriously compromised. Should the engine shortage ever increase to fourteen 'holes' then RAF Germany would no longer be able to meet SACEUR's requirement of 70 per cent force availability within twelve hours.

A working party was set up to look at the Phantom issue with the assumption that the absolute minimum flying hours for front line units would be 15 hours per crew per month. Its findings in early 1972 recommended that the total number of flying hours of the Phantom force be reduced to 1,890 hours per month. Because of a severe shortage of turbine blade material it was unlikely that Rolls-Royce would be able to improve on its current output of overhauled engines in the short term and so a drastic cutback in the amount of flying carried out was essential to prevent the AOG situation from getting even worse. The most difficult decision was how to implement a reduction in the overall flying task without affecting capability and unduly damaging the training organisation.

As already postulated, the chief cutbacks involved a reduction in aircraft strength of the three Air Support Command squadrons at Coningsby (Nos. 6, 41 and 54) together with a restriction in the total number of hours flown per month to 736 hours. The other major loser was the OCU which was restricted to essential flying only, i.e. the training of exchange officers and future squadron and flight commanders. Several courses had to be cancelled altogether, much to the disgust of pilots and navigators who had already completed the ground school, many of the latter group being shunted off to join the Vulcan force.

Eventually the Spey was made into a decent enough engine with acceptable Time Between Overhauls (TBOs), but the severe time and cost constraints that had been imposed during its inception had been a major factor in the engine's development problems and had not only resulted in greater expenditure in the long term, but had led to a potentially serious situation in that the RAF would have been sorely pressed to meet its requirements if it had been called upon. Undoubtedly the troubles at Rolls-Royce were also a factor in the length of time it took to solve the problems of the Spey 202, but they only served to compound a state of affairs that had at its root the political meddling in the defence industry in the 1960s.

CHAPTER FIVE

First Impressions

By the late 1960s the Phantom was already a legend in its own lifetime, thanks mainly to its exploits in the Vietnam War, so it was eagerly awaited by those RAF and Royal Navy crews lucky enough to have been selected to fly it. When the first Phantoms began to arrive for the RAF in 1968, Flight Lieutenant Peter Desmond was already a very experienced navigator with fifteen years service, mainly in the world of night/all-weather fighter operations. He began his 'love affair' with the F-4 in June 1969 during a three-year posting to A&AEE at Boscombe Down, primarily to work on the Phantom recce pod. Because of the late arrival of the latter, however, his tour was extended to four years and involved other flight testing.

The UK version of the Phantom represented a triumph of penny-pinching over experience. In order to succour Rolls-Royce, whose fortunes were tied up in the RB.211 then undergoing major teething troubles, it was decided to re-engine the F-4 with standard, proven Rolls-Royce Spey engines; these were in service with a number of airlines and were available off the shelf. They were economical in both price and performance and seemed preferable to the General Electric J79 that powered the US F-4. However, the Spey had no afterburner and to build a Mach 2 interceptor without reheat was unthinkable, so a bolt on reheat was designed to go on an engine which was never meant to have one. The initial version, which raised the thrust from 12,250 lb to 20,515 lb per engine, had a novel catalytic igniter system which took 5 seconds to ignite the stream of neat fuel poured into the after part of the jet exhaust, totally unacceptable to anyone who knows anything about flying heavyweight jets at low level or at slow speed, or both. Most low speed emergencies are over in 5 seconds, in fact, if they take longer than 5 seconds they are more likely to be a problem rather than an emergency. It took months of badgering before the project office agreed to update the stone-age igniter system to 1.4 seconds, the best they could do, which still seemed an age when an emergency took place.

The Spey engine was a bypass design which, by definition, was broader in the beam than a straightforward axial-flow engine, so the UK F-4 fuselage had to be made fatter than the US model which destroyed the area rule design that made the Phantom a Mach 2 fighter. The intake design also had to be changed to accommodate the Spey's increased appetite for air and this further lowered the performance. In fact, it was extremely rare for the UK F-4 to be flown at Mach 2. In addition, Ferranti had produced an inertial navigation system [INAS] which took 11 minutes for the primary gyro to align after engine start with the aircraft having to remain at a standstill (so much for the QRA alert status of 10 minutes readiness from alert to take-off). We decided to retrofit the INAS in service, which ultimately meant that nearly all the aircraft were at different modification states. However, this was a nightmare for the maintainers because the Line Replaceable Units (LRU) were different for each installation, so the spares stocking problem was immense. Fortunately they did not interfere with the radar or the missile system. If you wanted a brief on how to screw up a fine aeroplane, read the UK Phantom history!

Despite all that, I shall never forget my first sight of the F-4 and my first trip. I did a two-day course down at 'A' Squadron Aeroplane and Armament Experimental Establishment (A&AEE) followed by one day at Coningsby on the radar and that was it. My first flight in the Phantom was with Heinz Frick, a test pilot from 'A' Squadron (it was only his second), and occurred on 9 June 1969. The following day we carried out a dive bombing sortie on the Larkhill range which involved pitch in at 11,000 ft, a 40 degree dive angle, release at 6,500 ft, initiate pull-out not below 5,000 ft with a lowest planned height of 1,500 ft. It was almost unbelievable but that was the way things were done at Boscombe; if you were qualified to fly an aeroplane, you got on and flew it. On 17 July we went to Aldergrove to pick up the photo trials Phantom which was fitted with one of the first inertial navigation systems for the recce pod. The inertial platform took 20 minutes to align after engine start, instead of the published 11 minute wait, and I shall never forget the sight of the civilian groundcrew, with their duffel coat hoods up, looking for all the world like drenched gnomes, standing in the pouring rain, waiting for us to taxi.

My three years at Boscombe should have ended in 1969 but I was asked if I would stay on for a further year to start the trials on the Phantom recce pod which kept on slipping back in time. This was another British lash up and was made by EMI who had never made one before. It carried a range of sensors and cameras, including infra red linescan, sideways looking radar, day and night vertical and oblique cameras with image movement compensation for aircraft speed. It weighed 2,280 lb, was carried on the centreline station, which meant that you could not use the two forward Sparrow missiles which became 1,200 lb of useless dead weight and, worst of all, the recce pod could not be jettisoned in an emergency. The combination of a fixed one ton budgie on the centreline and 5 seconds light-up time on the afterburners was lethal. Everybody who flew it pointed this out to the project office but they insisted, saying that if it could be jettisoned, then someone would do it accidentally. It is a good job they did not apply the same argument to all the underwing and underbelly stores. We did not actually get the recce pod in the air until March 1970, approximately 18 months later than planned.

My final months at Boscombe were very pleasant and relaxed, flying in various aircraft including the Phantom on weapons carriage trials. One of these was quite interesting. When you flew carriage trials you had to land back at Boscombe with the particular test weapon load aboard and on one sortie we flew with 13 × 540 lb bombs which equates to 3 tons plus Sparrow missiles. Our touch-down speed was computed to be in excess of 160 knots, needless to say we made a very gentle approach and landing!

By the time the Phantom entered RAF squadron service in 1969 a number of pilots and navigators were already acquainted with the aircraft through exchange postings with the USAF and USMC. One of those was Flight Lieutenant (later Group Captain) Mike Shaw who flew F-4Bs with the US Marine Corps at Cherry Point, North Carolina.

The US Marines had a typically sink-or-swim approach to flying, which was not something I had met before my exchange tour in 1964–66. Before tackling the F-4B, I spent a useful month on VMT-7, a training squadron equipped with Grumman TF-9Js (two-seat Cougar – the 'Lead Sled') to familiarise myself with US Instrument Flying (IF) procedure. Pure IF was no problem as RAF standards match anyone's, but on Lightnings in the UK we had always done our best to avoid Airways, believing that fighters and airliners do not mix happily. In the US, it is different; the fighters use civil procedures and, on transit flights, the civilian controllers and Airways. It was an odd feeling to be overtaken, maybe 4,000 ft below, by a DC-8!

The first trip (or rather hop) in an F-4B was preceded by a week in ground school, along with trainee ground crew, followed by eight sessions in a Weapons System Trainer (WST). This was a bolted-to-the-floor simulator in a trailer manned by instructor Non-commissioned Officers (NCOs), but was perfectly adequate. The next step was a one-to-one discussion with the pilot detailed to fly the 'FAM' sortie with you, covering the relevant manual. He had probably overseen a final sortie in the WST, but had no idea of his student's flying ability. There were no dual-control F-4Bs, so the plan was to give the student a back-seat ride, to show him the aircraft's characteristics, then to land to refuel and change seats, before flying the same profile again with the student in the front.

And so it was with me. After the Lightning, the F-4B was a disappointment. It felt heavy, climbed slowly (400 kts IAS against the Lightning's 450 kts IAS) and buffeted at quite moderate angles of attack. In fact above 30,000 ft, subsonic, it wasn't really happy to turn at all. Designed to achieve the obligatory Mach 2, its thin wing had to be moving at 450 kts IAS or so before it could generate its full lift potential. This feature gave the aircraft a subsonic rate of turn which would beat an F-104, but not much else. This was improved in some later models by the introduction of leading edge slats (but not the UK's F-4K or F-4M). It clearly relied upon autostabilisation to fly smoothly, and the stick was too far forward for precise control. This became even more marked at high subsonic speed, as it moved with trim. It was not very comfortable and I was not impressed – at that stage. Then I went supersonic. First the afterburners and engine response, as a whole, were magnificent. Aircraft handling became easy, and the stick trimmed to where it should be, within reach. I was beginning to warm to the Phantom, particularly as, with 2 × 370 US gallon drop tanks, it had 2½ times the Lightning's fuel capacity with a similar consumption.

After returning to the 'pattern', or circuit, I put the gear (undercarriage) and flaps (Marines do occasionally speak English!) down, and once more found myself in a different flying machine. The stick was well aft, the aircraft felt rock solid and its controls and engines responded beautifully. It became clear why the Phantom was such a success as a carrier-borne aircraft. Landing was easy. The airframe was strong, with landing gear which could absorb the heaviest carrier landing loads. Its tailhook was stressed to 4½ g. As it could drop bombs and carry four Sidewinders (then AIM-9B) and four Sparrows (AIM-7E), with a good pulse radar (APQ-72), it was truly a multi-role combat aircraft.

Mike Shaw also comments on the layout of the Phantom cockpit which was rather more orderly than some British aircraft of the period, although certain switch positioning left a lot to be desired.

> In general the cockpit was well laid out and vision from the front seat was good – rather less so from the rear, which had a smaller canopy, heavy framing and the pilot's ejection seat all blocking the view. The engine intakes restricted the lateral vision from the back seat too, and landing a two-sticker from there demanded some skill. A strong crosswind would help, but not much. Even from the front seat there were blind spots behind the windscreen and canopy arches, necessitating sideways head movements to view the way ahead. It took the likes of the F-15 to overcome such shortcomings.
>
> The only switch that might have been better placed was that for the flaps, on the port front cockpit wall. It could be reached easily enough, but was near the handle for the Ram Air Turbine (RAT) which ran the emergency generator. On at least one occasion the position of the flap switch, which incorporated the emergency flap lever to blow down the flaps should the normal hydraulic system fail, led to the loss of a Phantom FGR.2. The pilot suffered a double generator failure one dark and dirty night, and selected emergency flaps instead of the RAT which would have powered the essential busbar to regain, inter alia, cockpit lightning, instruments and radio. This action induced a hydraulic failure and even more adrenaline. He had no wheel brakes, nosewheel steering or rudder, so when his hook failed to pick up the approach-end arrester wire, the aircraft veered off the runway. The navigator ejected, the pilot followed and both made it. The aircraft did not. What a pity that the switches/levers were so close together!

Squadron Leader (later Wing Commander) Anthony 'Bugs' Bendell was one of the first pilots to convert to the Phantom prior to becoming a Flight commander with Number 6 Squadron. Already an experienced pilot with three fighter tours behind him, including an exchange posting with the USAF as an instructor on the F-105 Thunderchief, Bendell first got his hands on a Phantom at 228 OCU Coningsby in early 1969. He recalled his impressions of the Phantom in his autobiography *Never In Anger* (Orion, 1998).

> The Phantom and the Lightning were about the same vintage, but while the Lightning had a certain elegance of line, the Phantom, with its cranked wings and anhedral stabilator, was just plain ugly. The anhedral stabilator was actually an effective alternative to the low-set

stabilators of both the Lightning and the F-105, but wiseacres would still claim that either McDonnell's chief designer had got his sums wrong or someone had trapped the tail in the hangar door.

The Rolls-Royce Spey engines each developed a nominal 20,000 lb of thrust in reheat – some 2,000 lb more than the General Electric J79 engines of the F-4J. The more powerful engines were essential to enable the Navy's Phantom FG.1s to operate from the relatively small British aircraft carriers – but at higher levels the hoped-for general improvement in performance was largely offset by a significant increase in aerodynamic drag. The fitting of the Speys to the RAF Phantoms was an expensive option which offered little if any real improvement. Compared to the F-4J, the UK Phantoms performed better on take-off and they had longer range, but they were slower at altitude. The massive tail hook and folding wings were clear evidence of the Phantom's naval pedigree. Less obvious, but essential to the aircraft's take-off and landing performance, was the use of boundary layer control. With BLC, high-pressure air, bled from the engines, was blown over the leading and trailing edge flaps to improve lift and reduce the minimum approach speed.

'The UK Phantoms were equipped with state-of-the-art ancillary equipment. The cockpit layout was typically American, with standard clock-face instrumentation. I recognised the ADI [Attitude Director Indicator] and the HSI [Horizontal Situation Indicator] from my F-105 flying, but there was the welcome addition of a radio altimeter. The Westinghouse/Ferranti AWG-12 pulse/Doppler radar more than doubled the range of previous British [Air Interception] AI radars, and provided an effective look-down capability. The communication fit was all British. The main radio was a combined UHF/VHF set offering some 28,000 manually dialled frequencies. The aircraft was also fitted with an HF radio for long-range work and a standby emergency radio. The FGR.2 was equipped with a Ferranti Inertial Nav/Attack System (INAS). In the navigation mode, the INAS's gyroscopically stabilised platform measured the aircraft's movement in space, which was then converted to ground speed and drift. This information was processed through a computer to update the aircraft's present position (presented in latitude and longitude) and gave course and distance to a number of pre-selected destinations. The FGR.2 was the first RAF fighter to be fitted with a self-contained, long-range navigation aid. With a good INAS, the typical error, after one hour in the air, was in the order of one nautical mile, but as it took a full year to iron out the problems with the INAS, our confidence in the equipment was slow to develop.

I flew my first Phantom solo with Dougie (Flight Lieutenant 'John' Douglas-Boyd) on 12 January 1969. The standard aircraft configuration at 228 OCU included two 308 imperial gallon 'Sergeant Fletcher' under-wing drop tanks, which more or less guaranteed a sortie duration of ninety minutes. It was easy to overlook this additional fuel load when comparing the Phantom's performance with previous aircraft. Certainly the Phantom accelerated faster than the F-105 on take-off, and it got airborne at a lower airspeed, but its performance was not as dramatic as the Lightning's and it was not as responsive on the controls. At speeds above 350 knots the Phantom handled well, but more care was needed when manoeuvring at lower speeds with higher angles of attack. The buffet margin, signifying an approaching stall, was never far away. Someone described the Phantom as wall-to-wall buffet; and after buffet came wing rock, which was a sure sign for the pilot to back off. At high AOA the Phantom was prone to adverse yaw (i.e. yawing away from the direction of turn), and at stalling speeds the aircraft could rapidly depart from normal flight. Intentional spinning was not recommended. Although it was possible to recover from a normal spin, the height lost per turn was in excess of 2,000 ft and there was always the possibility that the spin might become flat, from which there was no recovery.

The response of the Spey engine was slow for a fighter aircraft, and at high subsonic Mach numbers the large cross-section area at the tail pipes generated what the boffins called 'boat tail drag'. Unlike the Lightning at high altitude, the Phantom FGR.2 needed the assistance of gravity to accelerate to supersonic flight. The approved technique was to unload the aircraft (i.e. push the stick forward) into a shallow dive. Once through the high-drag transonic region the Phantom's handling improved, but it was still sluggish compared to the Lightning. In the landing configuration, with the benefit of an automatic aileron/rudder interconnect to compensate for adverse yaw, the aircraft was pleasantly stable. However, if the BLC malfunctioned the Phantom could be difficult to handle. Engine failure on take-off at a high all-up weight also required care and the asymmetric power was quite marked and had to be corrected. Despite its capricious handling characteristics, the F-4 Phantom was recognised as an extremely flexible multi-role combat aircraft.

The Phantom FGR.2 was best suited to pre-planned interdiction, where its superior range and navigation equipment could be used to advantage, rather than for close air support. Certainly compared to the Hunter, the Phantom, even with a partial load of air-to-air weapons, was better able to fend for itself behind enemy lines. Using the AWG-12's ground-mapping mode to let down through cloud in relative safety, we could press home our attack in far worse weather conditions. We used this tactic without a second thought, until we found that, due to an obscure technical fault, the radar picture could be off-set by as much as 30 degrees. Dougie and I had one close encounter with Exmoor when, according to the radar, we were letting down over the Bristol Channel. Other crews were similarly alarmed when they found discrepancies in the radar display but it was a simple matter to crosscheck the radar with the aircraft's other navigation aids.

For all the aircraft's sophistication, the FGR.2's conventional ground-attack weapons system was fairly basic. In the air-to-ground mode, the aiming pipper could be depressed to allow for the various weapons deliveries. The optical sight was effective when using forward-firing weapons such as the gun or SNEB rockets, but at low-grazing angles the radar ranging was not particularly accurate. The sighting problem was more difficult for dive bombing. To maintain a steady dive angle, the sight was allowed to drift on to the target. There was nothing new in this – it was the air-to-ground equivalent of pegged ranging. The sight depression varied according to the ballistics of the bomb, the speed of the aircraft and the desired height of release. But everything had to come together at the moment of bomb release; if any one of the parameters was adrift the bomb would miss the target, and even the minor errors tended to be cumulative. For example, a shallow dive angle would produce an early release sight picture at a lower than ideal airspeed and the bomb would fall many feet short of the target. In retrospect, it was remarkable that we ever scored a direct hit, especially when using an operational profile. The fact that we actually qualified in 20 degree free-fall dive bombing was a triumph of the old-fashioned seaman's eye – but that needed regular practice. Operational crews had to qualify across the whole range of conventional weaponry, including bombs, rockets and air-to-ground gunnery.

Apart from the weapons training, we practised simulated attack profiles using tactical formations of two or more aircraft. When short of aircraft, we would switch to singleton reconnaissance sorties using a strike camera mounted in the left forward Sparrow recess. Most of our flying was at low level, because, at that time, low altitude was believed to be the best way of avoiding detection by the Warsaw Pact's air defence radars. It took many months to optimise our tactics to make best use of the Phantom FGR.2's unique capabilities.

Chapter Six

The Phantom At Sea – An Artificer's View

Although the Royal Navy's original intention had been to form two squadrons of Phantoms to operate from the aircraft carriers HMS *Eagle* and HMS *Ark Royal*, Britain's declining interests abroad, together with escalating costs, resulted in a drastic pruning of the Phantom order and only 892 Squadron was to form aboard *Ark Royal.* The ship was to have been one of four 'Audacious' class carriers and was laid down by Cammell Laird at Birkenhead on 3 May 1943. Originally named *Irresistible*, the end of the Second World War meant that the order was reduced to just two carriers and it was renamed *Ark Royal*, with *Audacious* taking on the name *Eagle*. The ship was launched on 3 May 1950 and was finally completed on 25 February 1955. For the next twelve years it formed the spearhead of Royal Navy operations throughout the world.

In 1967 *Ark Royal* commenced a three year refit at Devonport so that it could operate the Phantom. The flight deck was increased in area (length 846 ft and beam 168 ft) and it was given a fully angled (8½ degree) deck. The old Mk.13 arresting gear was replaced by a direct-acting DA-2 water spray system which was needed to cater for the Phantom's higher landing weight and increased touchdown speed. Of the two forward catapults, that on the starboard bow was removed and a replacement located on the angled deck. Following damage to the decks of US aircraft carriers caused by increased jet blast and higher exhaust temperatures of the Phantom FG.1, special water-cooled 8 ft high blast deflectors were installed at each catapult point, together with deck cooling plates. As the launching bridle for the Phantom was considerably more expensive than that utilised for previous types such as the Sea Vixen and Buccaneer, an arrester was incorporated in an elongated extension ahead of each catapult so that it could be reused. A further reason for this system being adopted was that it was possible, under certain conditions, for the bridle to foul the Phantom's external stores. Following its refit *Ark Royal* underwent catapult calibration tests in Lyme Bay off the Dorset coast before being declared fully operational.

The arrival of the Phantom into Fleet Air Arm service brought added responsibility for Lionel Smith, an artificer, who was to be tasked with keeping the aircraft operational during *Ark Royal*'s first cruise to the Caribbean and the eastern seaboard of the USA. He recalls some of his work at that time and a few of the difficulties he encountered maintaining the Phantom, both on land and at sea.

When the Phantoms started to arrive in 1968 I was based at RNAS Yeovilton. At that time we were working seven days a week, and as many hours a day as it took, to complete the heavy modification programme. The Rolls-Royce Spey went through numerous updates so we were always pulling and replacing engines. This meant a long walk across to the far side of the airfield to the V-bomber dispersals and then hours in the open air doing ground runs. During the first rapid reheat test we had an engine 'banger'. This was caused by afterburner overfuel due to reduced airflow from boundary layer bleed and the fuel control not compensating enough. A large cloud of unburnt AVCAT fuel would build up behind the aircraft and then suddenly ignite. Fire extinguishers would be knocked over like skittles and the perspex windows in the side of the crew van were blown out by the shock wave. Rolls-Royce would not believe us until one of their engineers had actually witnessed this for himself.

A similar reheat bang occurred whilst a Phantom was on the deck-hook hold back point on Fly-4 on *Ark Royal* having a rapid reheat test on a newly installed engine. The bang caused the engine to shift in its bearings enough to unship the main fuel inlet manifold, a 4 in diameter pipe with about 400psi pressure (reheat was one of the states which ensured that all fuel pumps, the electrically driven boost pumps in the No. 1 tanks and the hydraulically driven pumps in some rear tanks, were running). This had potentially disastrous consequences as fuel washed down over the edges of the flight deck and onto open decks below, but luckily no harm was done.

One of the modifications installed on the naval Phantoms was the APCS (Automatic Power Compensation System). This was fitted to ensure minimum stagger between the port and starboard throttle levers on a deck approach. As engineers we were required to ground run both engines and soak them. A special block with graduations marked on it (rather like a rule) was positioned between the throttle levers and the engines would be accelerated up to 90 per cent in stages, allowing rpm to stabilise at each chosen value and positions of the throttle markers noted on a knee pad. APCS checks became interesting during a brief spell ashore at the time Rolls-Royce was in financial difficulty. We were very short of replacement engines and Rolls only had enough to be sent to the ship as spares for the next deployment. So we airframe and engines chaps (this is a dual trade in the FAA) had so many engine runs to do that all the attenuators and chocks were in use. Having both Spey engines at about 90 per cent power long enough to stabilise rpm and take readings of TGT and throttle positions was not for the faint of heart and, even with chained pairs of chocks on each of the three wheels, the aircraft would begin to roll!

Operationally we used a policy of flexible servicing based on calendar, flying hours, running hours (engines and some associated ancillary units), or landings as appropriate. With respect to tyres, the number of deck landings allowed was higher than those ashore because there was less wear on deck landings. One of our Phantoms (XV565/001) ditched off the Florida coast on 29 June 1971 and a replacement from 767 Squadron (XT868) was flown out to *Ark Royal* as we were in the western approaches. This aircraft required some work to make it carrier operational, both main wheel tyres, for example, had been on a 'one flight only' restriction. On return to home waters, instead of flying off the Air Group and entering port, Exercise *Limelight* intervened. This was to be the live televising, for an episode of Tomorrows World, of RN carrier operations with commentary by the renowned Raymond Baxter.

During the period of actual broadcasting of the programme we had an urgent operational requirement to get XT868 ranged on deck and ready for flying off with the rest of the squadron to Yeovilton as soon as the broadcast was over. Unfortunately, I had very little time (under ten minutes) to change both main wheels ready for the manglers (aircraft handlers) to tow it to the for'ard lift and so to the flight deck. Full aircraft jacking would have taken too long so I detailed two teams from the best hands in the watch and used single wheel jacking by turn on each side with myself carefully orchestrating the timing and doing the appropriate checks when required. The actual process was done in under five minutes. There was a TV screen mounted in the hangar so that we could see what was being broadcast. I was amused to see that at the moment XT868 should have been arising to deck level, there was a bows shot of Ark with no aircraft making a slow appearance above flight deck level, so 'live' broadcast was a slight exaggeration. One half of the forward section of the hangar was filled with outside broadcast vans with large bundles of cables running through the armoured door track so that it could not be closed off in the event of an emergency. This amazed us at the time as it breached all the fire and safety regulations normally in force.

REPLACING ENGINES

The Spey engine was quite a tight fit and required more than a little manoeuvring in the vertical and horizontal planes and adjustments to the fore-and-aft angle of presentation whilst being rolled in or out of the airframe in what was something of a tortuous path to avoid obstacles protruding into the engine bay. To achieve this, the roll in/out stand was equipped with a single pillar at the front and a pillar each side towards the rear, each having a hoisting mechanism attached to the engine. The initial aligning could make or break the roll in and had to take account of any ring bolts in the deck along the way. Usually a team of six was employed on a roll in, although four could do it at a squeeze, plus the senior rate in charge. One essential watcher, by choice an experienced chap, would be positioned in the intake and, if available, one on each side of the engine. There would also be one on each pillar to lower or hoist as required. Only when all was ready would the drop-out link, connecting the lower keel to the wing root and carrying the already disconnected aileron droop walking beam control cable, be removed. It was mandatory to refit drop-out links immediately on fitting or removing an engine to prevent the fuselage distorting or splaying.

The chain lashings used at the time were not ideal for every task. I recall a Phantom Spey engine on a transportation stand breaking free of the lashings as movement caused individual links to twist and take up new positions, thus causing slack in the whole. The engine then proceeded to charge backwards and forwards along the hangar deck as the ship pitched, with the forward limit of roll getting ever closer to the for'ard lift with each pitch. Fortunately, we managed to impede its progress and arrest its movement before it could fall to the hangar deck level below. After this episode I could at least assimilate with the sailors of old, wrestling with a loose cannon in the seaway of one of Nelson's warships!

AIRCRAFT JACKING AT SEA

This was necessarily a more troublesome, and hazardous, activity at sea involving more hands to look after loosening of lashings as the aircraft rose, as well as pump and wind down the collars of the jacks. A three-point jacking required all jacks to be positioned under the aircraft's jacking points (this could be troublesome if a ring bolt or two happened to be where jack feet were placed), jacking pads were inserted and the jacks slowly extended to close the gap and ensure correct alignment with the points. Then all jacks were lashed to ring-bolts in the deck. All members of the jacking party then stood by whilst the senior rating dashed quickly into the squadron hangar maintenance office and telephoned the ships bridge to seek permission to jack one Phantom. At times a wait was involved until the watch crew were certain that a steady course was going to be steered for long enough to complete the jacking operation.

I recall one occasion where I had obtained permission and had only time to detail the slackening of the aircraft's lashings when my senses told me that the ship was heeling. I quickly barked an order to secure lashings and ducked back into the office to telephone the bridge and enquire (forcefully) what was going on. On securing the aircraft once jacked up, and with another jack and pad positioned securely under the keel just for'ard of the deck-hook attachment position, another phone call to the bridge was made to advise that the jacking operation was complete.

NOSE UNDERCARRIAGE EMERGENCY SHRINK TEST

This particular operation, whereby the 40 in nose leg extension was shrunk by the use of air from the aircraft's pneumatic system if the normal hydraulic shrink had failed, was quite interesting. A rating was required to take up position in the cockpit to operate the selection controls. He was instructed to close the canopies to avoid straining the hinge and operating mechanism, and also for his own safety so that he was not thrown clear of the cockpit when selecting emergency shrink. This latter consideration was because the leg shrunk so quickly that the aircraft nose was momentarily suspended before gravity took charge. Indeed the nose dropped so rapidly that the main wheels would often jump high enough off the deck to clear the chocks. This was accompanied by a very surprised look on the face of the rating in the cockpit if this was his first acquaintance with the phenomenon.

Ashore it was policy to pull the aircraft forward to allow enough space at the rear so as not to cause a collision with the hangar wall. At sea this was not an option and additionally, because of the degree of rotation and movement at all undercarriage positions, no nose lashings were feasible and those at the main legs were slackened off to prevent damage as they would be drawn tighter. This hazardous operation was, necessarily, followed by much filling and bleeding of the nose undercarriage hydraulic system to ensure that all the air was removed (frothy strawberry mousse by the bucket full!).

The emergency shrink and vent valve was located at the rear of the bay enclosed by 'panel 6 right' which contained the cabin air conditioning system ('panel 6 left' covered the bay housing the avionics conditioning systems, these being fed air through the small chin intakes just aft of the radome). The bay under 6 right was a veritable Chinese puzzle of pipelines, control valves, exchangers and cables, most of which had to be removed to get access for changing a faulty shrink and vent valve. You can imagine the chagrin when, having fitted a replacement valve, refitted all the surrounding equipment and then proceeded with the shrink test, it was then discovered that the new valve was also unserviceable! The only practical way we had of testing these valves was in situ, i.e. on the aircraft. This particular scenario was not uncommon as many of the new valves arriving from the US were u/s.

One night-watch (the 1800–0730 that we dubbed the 'doom watch') during an unusually quiet spell I decided to dig through the servicing manuals and by studying the electrical and pneumatic/hydraulic systems as a whole, I was able to come up with a way to inhibit, using rear cockpit circuit breakers and/or gagging microswitches, some of the actions of the system. This allowed a partial test to be carried out that saved a lot of time and hydraulic fluid. Having found a way, I ran the idea past an electrical artificer who agreed that it made sense. We were unable to adopt the routine at the time but I believe that it did later become standard practice. I also suggested to one of the AEOs (Air Engineering Officers) that if the shrink and vent valve was moved to the aft side of the bulkhead to which it was mounted (in a small clear space above and ahead of the forward starboard Sparrow receptacle) that all the hassle associated with dismantling the cabin conditioning system could be avoided. As far as I know, this was also done later.

Reheat, Fuel Leaks and Engine Tests

In the very early days of modifying engines at Yeovilton one requirement was to remove the internal components of a redundant valve unit situated on the underside of the engine just forward of the jet pipe and replace the cover with a new seal. It was required that a visual check be made of this valve for absence of leaks during the next afterburner run. This could only be done by crawling and backsliding into position under the engine whilst it was running, with the face only inches below the valve. The unfortunate person then had to remain under the engine whilst reheat was engaged to check for leaks. What fun that was!

Also at that time it was required to run the engines with test sets connected. The chap in the cockpit was mostly there just to start up and shut down, and to select the flaps etc. The supervisor on the test set would flick switches and rotate control wheels to accelerate and decelerate the engine whilst watching various meters on the set. This was one thing ashore, but on board ship strange things began to happen. With the engine running under test set control, accelerations and decelerations were occurring with no input from either the test set operator or the guy in the cockpit. This caused a lot of head scratching as no one really knew what was going on. It transpired that signals were being induced in the connecting cables as the crew moved through the ship, opening and closing doors and hatches and disturbing the ship's magnetic field. Somebody had the bright idea of visiting the ship's galley and 'razzing' loads of cooking foil which was wrapped around the cable run as shielding. Amazingly, it worked!

Of Manglers, Stabilators and Drill Bits

The conditions we had to work in were often extremely difficult and most uncomfortable. On one occasion during the usual late evening shift 'elephant tango' (idiom for the aircraft shuffle) on the flight deck, a mangler managed to drive his fork-lift truck into the port inboard trailing edge of the stabilator of one of our Phantoms. It was subsequently decided that, as we had the component in stock, we would change just that one inboard honeycomb section. This section was attached at the top and bottom surface and at the stabilator main spar by Jo-Bolts, a patent type of fastener with, in this case, high tensile steel central mandrills. Unfortunately, these presented a problem in that we had a shortfall of the necessary diamond tipped drills as a result of cost cutting. So drilling these mandrills was rather laborious and very tiring.

It was a typically hot and humid tropical night in the Caribbean with temperatures in the upper hangar well above 120°F. Even so, we were slightly better off than out counterparts on 809 Squadron Buccaneers in the lower hangar. There were two of us involved, both dressed in shorts, sandals and with sweat rags around forehead, wrists and waists (looking almost like a couple of Buccaneers ourselves). Access to the inboard Jo-Bolts was restricted. The distance between the underside of the stabilator and the fuselage at the inboard end was so short that specially cut down, and reground, bits in a right-angled windy drill could only be used. I had a pocket full of these short drills specially ground slightly off centre so as to chip away at the mandrill because the soft bit-material had no chance of a normal cut. The chippings falling onto my bare and sweating chest sent up dozens of vapour wisps, accompanied by a sizzling sound, as I worked.

Every so often I would have to change the drill bit and then break for longer to take the long walk to the Air Engineering workshops in front of the for'ard aircraft lift and hangar extension to grind the tips of the bits back into useful form. Working on Phantoms certainly ensured that you acquire the knack of grinding small drills on the workshop grindstone. The chap working on the upper surface had a different problem as he was forced to hook on with one hand whilst drilling with the other due to the anhedral nature of the stabilator (the normal servicing platform could not be used as it would have obscured the inboard upper Jo-Bolts). Because of the uncomfortable nature of each position we swapped periodically. In spite of the sweat rags, a large pool of moisture formed on the hangar deck below the stabilator's port tip. Happy days!

OF ACCESS PANELS AND NUMEROUS FASTENERS

There were many large panels on the Phantom that required frequent removal for servicing. Four are particularly memorable, 36 left and right, and 111 left and right. Panels 36 left and right were situated on the vertical fuselage side in the region of the upper mainplane undercarriage bulge. With these removed the stresses on the aircraft were such that it was mandatory to position a support trestle under the keel, just forward of the deck-hook hinge. Panels 111 left and right were situated on the upper surface of the outboard folding wing sections, just aft of the leading edge flaps. These had to be removed on a regular basis for flap link greasing. Each panel 111 had a total of 948 fasteners. These were mostly close tolerance HTS [High Tensile Steel] countersunk headed bolts (as with 36 left and right) which under the stresses of flight often seized in and required various degrees of coercion to shift. It was not uncommon to have about 10 per cent which needed to be drilled out. That may not sound many, but 10 per cent of 948 is still 94 and that represented a lot of drilling. For this one servicing operation we thus had to remove 1,896 fasteners on each and every aircraft on the squadron, every twenty-one days or so. When we first went to sea with Phantoms we were woefully under provisioned with replacement fasteners of all types. The situation became so bad that we often had to seek clearance to allow flying with a certain percentage missing or borrow some from other aircraft, our two 'hangar queens' (sometimes referred to as Christmas Trees) which were gradually being stripped for spares.

Of Heavy Landings, Undercarriage Doors and Arrester Wires

On board *Ark Royal* we seemed to have periods, often in humid conditions, where aircraft would depart from the usual plan of a controlled crash at catching a wire and thump down hard enough to blow both main wheels. The results were dire. The spreading tyre material would remove undercarriage fairings and the pipe runs (hydraulic and pneumatic) fitted to the main landing strut. At one time we were so short of doors that a special local repair, using stainless steel patches, was worked on doors not totally destroyed. I recall that we put in a stores demand for some replacement doors after using up all the spares on the ship. The only ones available were at RAF Bruggen and we were in the Florida-Puerto Rico area at the time. After following us around the Caribbean we eventually collected these from a supply ship whilst not far from the Lizard on our way home.

I also recall a time when our Phantoms were pulling the arrester wires out of their mountings. The runs of these went along the outboard deck-head of the upper hangar. The noise and vibration as this happened was quite startling, for the first time at least. On one occasion I was just exiting the port midships air-lock access into the hangar itself as a wire was pulled right out. The vibration through the ship's structure was enough to dislodge a dockyard workers lead mallet head that had been discarded. It plunged down striking the forward sloping Sidewinder missile pylon on one aircraft and ricocheted in my direction. I ducked and it shot over my head. On another occasion a large engineer's square plunged onto the inboard trailing edge flap (aluminium honeycomb) of one of our Phantoms. Fortunately it fell flat and so caused little damage.

On Engine Burner Cleaning and Gas Turbine Starters

When the Phantom first entered service we had a lot of trouble with the Plessey Solent Gas Turbine Starters (GTS). There were a number of occasions where the guts of these disintegrated and were blown out of the downturned exhausts in a shower of sparks, spouts of flame and clouds of smoke. It was not a total surprise to us that a gas turbine engine rotating at about 75,000 rpm and required to output 92shp should occasionally behave in this way. Fortunately they were not large, about 11 inches in diameter and about 18 inches long (including the exhaust nozzle), so replacing starters was not too taxing, although one always breathed a sigh of relief once the new turbine was clamped firmly enough to be able to let go of it, as they were structurally quite dense.

I recall having to change the port GTS on 003 (XT861) ashore in Puerto Rico in 1971. At that time centreline tanks were fitted to all aircraft. To remove the port GTS the forward auxiliary air door had to be removed. This was attached at its inboard, upper end by a piano hinge. The long wire of this hinge terminated after a right angled bend which was positively locked into place by an overlying top hat section sheet metal clamp secured by a pair of 10 UNF bolts. Access to this top hat bracket was via a panel which hinged down and outwards but which could only be moved out of the way in the absence of the centreline tank. It turned out that 003 was the only aircraft that had not had this top hat bracket 'modified' (unofficially) to aid dislocation so as to withdraw the auxiliary air door pin with the tank still in place. As I had no armourers ashore with me, removing the tank was not an option but, somehow, I managed.

To give an idea of the things that we had to put up with, the mole grips that I had taken ashore with me were so worn, and with loose jaw pieces, as to be virtually useless in the circumstances. Using my initiative I visited the US tool shack, showed my grips to the staff and asked if they had anything similar (but in good condition) that I could borrow. 'Sure, how many do you want?' was the reply, which only served to show the difference in philosophy between the two national services.

By the time we reached the end of our first deployment to the Caribbean both of our 'hangar queens' on *Ark Royal* lacked, amongst other things, gas turbine starters. A stores demand had been placed for six additional spare units some time prior to reaching this particular state. Imagine our relief when, following replenishment, six crates duly appeared in our hangar. The relief was short lived, however, for each one proved to contain a starter for the sole Gannet COD aircraft that we had on board, the starters of which required replacing once every other blue moon. A stores system operative had managed to request the wrong reference number, not unprecedented, but certainly awkward in this case. It was a good thing that there wasn't a (hot) war on at the time!

The ground running of engines could be a dangerous business for all involved. LIX washing of the engine burners was a requirement because of the dirty burning of the AVCAT fuel that was used. This type of fuel was preferred for carrier use, and for Royal Navy aircraft ashore, because of its higher flashpoint but, more importantly, because it did not promote the growth of a particular fungus in the storage tanks of the ship, or air station for that matter. Having worked on the fuel storage facilities at Yeovilton as part of my 'in field' training as an apprentice Aircraft Artificer, I was aware that we kept other fuels such as AVTUR and AVTAG, visiting aircraft for the use of.

One dark, wet and windy night at Yeovilton during the period when Rolls-Royce was in trouble, we were trying hard to fix every troublesome Spey engine on the Phantoms without going as far as replacement. It had been decided that in the event of engines not reaching self sustaining rpm after a LIX wash that another LIX wash should be carried out followed by the customary 'soak' period and then another ground run. At a watch changeover I took over on one aircraft from a colleague who had carried out a LIX wash on both engines. I still had a couple of hours to wait for the LIX to take effect so in the meantime I carried out a nose leg change on another aircraft. In due course I gave the first aircraft its engine runs but neither engine would reach self sustaining rpm (it was a near run thing with the port engine) and on shutdown considerable quantities of unburned AVCAT poured out of the jet pipes onto the concrete. The aircraft was moved to the other end of the flight line and the station fire crews invited to come and hose down the spillage.

Another LIX wash was carried out on both engines. After the customary soak period I started up the port engine which, with a little encouragement, reached self sustaining rpm. The starboard engine, however, proved to be rather more recalcitrant. Despite only operating the gas turbine starter for its allotted time, and only once at that, it decided that it had had enough and exploded in spectacular fashion, or so I was told. From my position in the cockpit I could not really see what was going on at the back, but the look on the face of my assistant and the speed with which he grabbed a fire extinguisher suggested that the aircraft was on fire. I also noticed the ground crew on an adjacent cab (in the Royal Navy aircraft were called 'cabs' by all and not 'kites' as in the RAF) suddenly rushing to the rear of my aircraft with extinguishers as unburned fuel from the combustion chambers had ignited in the jet pipe of the starboard Spey. I decided at that point that it was about time to shut down the port Spey and make a hasty exit from the cockpit!

Lionel Smith's involvement with the Phantom came to an end in the mid-1970s when he had to retire from active service due to spinal injuries. Despite this he put in many more years of valuable service with the Naval Aircraft Trial Installation Unit (NATIU) where he worked on a wide variety of aircraft including Hunter, Sea King, Lynx, Wessex, Wasp, Sea Devon and Canberra. Although he harboured a desire to work on the Phantom once again, it was not to be and the aircraft left naval service in 1978 when *Ark Royal* was taken out of service. All remaining Royal Navy Phantoms were transferred to the RAF where they were eventually taken on by 111 Squadron at Leuchars. Over the next ten years Phantom FG.1s flown by 43 and 111 Squadrons covered the northern area of the UK Air Defence Region, until replaced by the Tornado F.3 from September 1989.

CHAPTER SEVEN

Phantom Tactics – Penetration

When the Phantom FGR.2 began to enter service with the RAF's front line units from 1969 it did so primarily in the strike, ground attack and tactical reconnaissance roles, the first deliveries being made to 6 Squadron at Coningsby which was soon joined by 54 Squadron. The first deliveries for RAF Germany were made in July 1970 and over the next twelve months the Bruggen Wing (Nos. 14, 17 and 31 Squadrons) was built up to form the RAF's main offensive element in 2ATAF. Suitable tactics had to be devised quickly so that the Phantom could be used effectively against Warsaw Pact forces and to this end a study was conducted by the Central Tactics and Trials Organisation (CTTO) at High Wycombe.

In the event of war in Europe it was envisaged that the Bruggen Wing would operate from its home base, with the Phantom squadrons of Air Support Command deploying to Wildenrath, these two being the only airfields that were equipped to handle the Phantom and its weapons loads in 2ATAF. The plan for conventional war was divided into four main programmes, Pre-planned Counter Air (PPCA), Interdiction and Armed Reconnaissance east and west of the peacetime Demarcation Line (IE and IW) and Close Support. For PPCA it was considered that attacks on targets such as runways and hangarettes would not lead to profitable results so the primary attacks would be against aircraft in the open, the control elements of air defence radars and missile systems. Should SACEUR direct that the PPCA programme be carried out, the Phantoms were to launch attacks on their pre-planned targets up to a radius of 240 nm from their operating airfields. For IE and IW missions the main targets were to be choke points, such as approach roads to bridges, which would give the best opportunity to destroy armour. Close air support was very much a secondary mission for the Phantom and was only to be

1. The first Phantom was the McDonnell XFD-1 (later FH-1) powered by two Westinghouse J30 turbojets of 1,600 lb thrust which endowed a top speed of 479 mph. It was only built in small numbers but achieved distinction in becoming the first US Navy jet to be cleared for carrier operations. *(Philip Jarrett)*

2. McDonnell F4H-1F Phantom 142260 took part in the US Marine Corps Skyburner project. Flown by Lt Col R. B. Robinson, it achieved a World Absolute Speed Record of 1606.51mph (Mach 2.59) on 22 November 1961. *(Philip Jarrett)*

3. An F-4B Phantom of VF-96 Fighting Falcons blasts off from the deck of USS *Ranger*. *(Philip Jarrett)*

4. The prototype F-4J (153072) is taken into the air on its maiden flight on 27 May 1966. The J was a heavily revised version of the basic F-4B and featured uprated J79 engines, together with much improved systems. *(Philip Jarrett)*

5. The first YF-4K (XT595) was first flown on 27 June 1966 with McDonnell test pilot Joe Dobronski at the controls. The first of two YF-4K development machines, the aircraft was demonstrated to a large crowd of British and US defence dignitaries at St Louis the following day. *(Philip Jarrett)*

6. Phantom FG.1 XT857 gets airbourne from HMS *Eagle* during the main carrier trials which were performed in June 1969. *(Philip Jarrett)*

7. Phantom FG.1 XT859 '725' of 700P Squadron overflies HMS *Hermes* in 1968 at the start of the carrier's new commission. *(Philip Jarrett)*

8. Phantom FG.1 XT870 '010' of 892 Squadron in clean configuration during a low-level, high-speed demonstration. *(Philip Jarrett)*

9. A head-on view of a Phantom FG.1 showing the outer wings folded and enlarged air intakes to cater for the increased mass flow of the Spey engines. *(Philip Jarrett)*

10. Royal Navy Phantom crews were brought up to operational standard by 767 Squadron at Yeovilton. One of the aircraft flown by this unit was XT864 '151'. *(Philip Jarrett)*

11. A Phantom FG.1 of 892 Squadron is manhandled into place on the catapult of the USS *Saratoga*. The deck plates of the *Saratoga* suffered greatly due to the higher exhaust temperatures of the Spey-Phantom and its more tail-down attitude. *(Philip Jarrett)*

12. Dramatic view of a Phantom FG.1 of 892 Squadron about to take a wire on HMS *Ark Royal*. *(Philip Jarrett)*

13. Another view of XT859 '725' which was the solo display aircraft at the 1968 Farnborough Air Show. *(Philip Jarrett)*

14. The Phantom's multi-role capability is highlighted in this view of an FG.1 of 892 Squadron leaving the deck of HMS *Ark Royal* with a load of 1,000 lb bombs. *(Philip Jarrett)*

15. Close up of the Rolls-Royce Spey engine that powered the RAF/RN Phantom. Technical difficulties with the reheat system and turbine blade failures caused serviceability rates to plummet. *(Philip Jarrett)*

16. Phantom FG.1 XT858 undergoes reheat trials. This was the aircraft used by Lt Cdr Brian Davies, O.C. 892 Squadron, and Lt Cdr Peter Goddard to set the fastest overall time of 5 hr 11 min 22 sec during the Daily Mail Transatlantic Air Race in May 1969. *(Philip Jarrett)*

17. Two of 767 Squadron's Phantom FG.1s. The lead aircraft is XT866 which survived until 9 July 1981 when it crashed following instrument failure on a night approach to Leuchars when serving with 43 Squadron. *(Philip Jarrett)*

18. A Phantom FG.1 of 892 Squadron blasts off from the deck of HMS *Ark Royal.* *(Lionel Smith)*

19. XT852 was the first YF-4M and was flown for the first time at St Louis on 17 February 1967. *(Philip Jarrett)*

20. Another view of XT852 in the air. *(Philip Jarrett)*

21. The first production Phantom FGR.2 (XT891) shows off its underwing and centreline fuel tanks. A twin-stick aircraft, XT891 arrived at 23 MU Aldergrove on 20 July 1968 and was delivered to 228 OCU at Coningsby a month later. *(Philip Jarrett)*

22. FGR.2 XV486 of 14 Squadron is seen here with Jaguar GR.1 XX762 in April 1975 when the Bruggen-based unit replaced its Phantoms with the Anglo-French aircraft in the ground attack role. *(Philip Jarrett)*

23. Phantom FGR.2 XV424 carried special markings in 1979 to commemorate the sixtieth anniversary of the first non-stop transatlantic flight by Capt John Alcock and Lt Arthur Whitten Brown. It was flown by Sqn Ldr Tony Alcock (nephew of John Alcock) and Flt Lt W. N. Browne (no relation). *(Philip Jarrett)*

24. The first major Phantom variant to be flown by the USAF was the F-4C. This is 64-0661 of the 110th Tactical Fighter Squadron, Missouri Air National Guard, seen during a detachment at Leeming on 30 June 1982. *(P. R. Caygill collection)*

25. The multi-role Phantom was equally at home when tasked with photo reconnaissance. This USAF RF-4C (69-0382) wears the black fin stripe of the 1st Tactical Reconnaissance Squadron, 10th Tactical Reconnaissance Wing. Normally based at Alconbury, it is seen here at Upper Heyford. *(P. R. Caygill collection)*

26. This F-4F Phantom (37+44) was one of 175 such aircraft delivered to the *Luftwaffe* and was photographed at Alconbury in 1982. *(P. R. Caygill collection)*

27. Phantom FGR.2 (XV407) of 41 Squadron, shown carrying a wide variety of stores comprising four Sparrow AAMs, two underwing fuel tanks, four BL 755 Cluster Bombs and a recce pod. *(Philip Jarrett)*

28. Phantom FGR.2 XV433 of 228 OCU sports its new all grey colour scheme at Binbrook in 1982. *(P. R. Caygill collection)*

employed if the enemy advance could not be contained, or if political constraints precluded operations east of the Demarcation Line.

In common with all aircraft carrying external stores, the Phantom suffered significantly increased drag which limited speed and increased fuel consumption for any given speed. Although it was possible for the Phantom FGR.2 to carry a total of 11 × 1,000 lb bombs, such a load limited the aircraft to internal fuel only and this, together with the high drag of the bombs and their suspension equipment, limited the operational radius to 115 nm which was insufficient even to reach the Demarcation Line. Thus for any practical penetration profile at low level it was necessary to carry external fuel tanks and accept a smaller weapons load. The Phantom could accept wing tanks totalling 4,872 lb of usable fuel and/or a centreline tank of 3,950 lb. Wing tanks were generally favoured as, although they imposed a slightly higher drag factor, they gave more usable fuel and were less restrictive as regards the aircraft's 'g' limitations. The fitment of a centreline tank also imposed a large time penalty should it be necessary to convert to the nuclear role and, when used in conjunction with under-wing tanks and an offensive load of 4 × 1,000 lb bombs, tended to raise AUW above the permitted maximum which placed take-off speed very close to the nose and main wheel limiting speed.

The four preferred weapons configurations were as follows:

Weapon Load	Usable fuel lb	Penetration drag No.	AUW lb
4 × 1,000 lb retard bomb 1 × SUU-23 gun pod 2 × Sparrow missiles	17,979	71	58,154
4 × cluster weapon 1 × SUU-23 gun pod 2 × Sparrow missiles	17,979	71	56,034
4 × Matra 155 (SNEB) 1 × SUU-23 gun pod 2 × Sparrow missiles	17,979	58.2	55,210
6 × Lepus flare 1 × SUU-23 gun pod 2 × Sparrow missiles	17,979	48.6	54,338

Use of the SUU-23 gun pod provided the Phantom with an air-to-ground weapons system, thus allowing the option of attacking soft skinned targets. It also improved the chances of survival if attacked by fighter aircraft. However, these advantages had to be set against increased weight and drag which resulted in a range penalty of about 15 nm radius of action. In general, unless special considerations applied, such as the need for the carriage of a centreline fuel tank for extended range, it was considered better to choose the additional offensive and defensive capability provided by use of the gun pod.

While seeking to employ the highest possible speed in the low level attack role to minimise exposure time to ground defences, the possible speed range of the FGR.2 during *en route* penetration was 360 to 480 knots. From the point of view of acceptable fuel consumption, however, the practical choice of speed lay between 360 and 420 knots. Assuming a drag index of 65, which was a representative figure with the range of weapons loads under consideration, there was a 16 per cent increase in fuel consumption from 360 to 420 knots. As Bruggen and Wildenrath were the two most westerly airfields in 2ATAF the first 180 nm of any mission was flown over friendly territory and so a considerable fuel saving could be made by flying at the slower speed on this part of the mission. The theoretical saving (AUW 45,000 lb and ICAN sea level conditions) is shown below.

Speed kts	Distance nm	Time mins	Fuel consumption lb/min	Fuel Used lb
360	180	30	157	4,710
420	180	25.75	211	5,433

The fuel saving of 723 lb was considered to be significant and represented about 50 seconds in full reheat which for any mission into East Germany could well mean the difference between success and failure. For this reason 360 knots was recommended for the initial phase of all attack sorties, with an increase of speed to 420 knots before penetrating hostile airspace. In the weapons configurations proposed, the FGR.2 was restricted in range to such an extent that the depth of penetration into East Germany would have been very limited. For some PPCA targets squadron commanders would have had to choose between reducing the weapons load, or accepting sorties without any combat fuel allowance. However, many tactics advisors at the time were of the opinion that any large scale movement by Warsaw Pact forces would lead to a rapid advance westwards, so that any shortcomings in the Phantom's range would soon become immaterial as its roles would be quickly transformed into interdiction and close support conducted entirely over West German territory.

Another issue which had to be given high priority when considering Phantom operations in northern Europe was the weather factor. A statistical study of the weather over the north German plain showed that conditions of 500 ft cloud base and two miles visibility were exceeded 90 per cent of the year, varying from 70 per cent in winter to 95 per cent in summer. A study of weather likely to be encountered over East Germany showed similar cloud base figures, but a significantly better visibility record due, it was thought, to lower levels of pollution.

In terms of navigation capability, a fully equipped Phantom FGR.2 was fitted with an Inertial Navigation Attack System (INAS), AWG-12 radar, STR-70 radio altimeter, Tactical Air Navigation System (TACAN) and AN-AJB/7 Attitude Reference Set. At the time that the CTTO report was compiled the majority of Air Support Command Phantoms had not been fitted with INAS but a retrofit programme was well under way which was eventually completed by the end of 1972. When fitted, INAS provided the navigator with information relating to aircraft attitude, track and heading, present position in latitude and longitude, groundspeed and range and bearing to a stored destination.

Although it was primarily an airborne interception radar and missile control system, the AWG-12 also had a ground mapping capability and the 25 nm scale, which was roughly equivalent to 1:500,000 mapping, could be used for *en route* navigation. The display was track-stabilised in INAS-equipped aircraft, and the INAS also provided the facility to position cursors on the radar display at the computed position of a stored destination. The AN-AJB/7 Attitude Reference Set was the primary attitude and heading reference on aircraft that had not yet been fitted with INAS and became a standby system after they were so fitted. The system had no acceleration or turn cut-outs so that after a steep turn the indicated heading would be in error for a short time by anything up to 5 degrees.

Visual navigation was normally practised by Phantom crews at 250 ft AGL and 420 knots, although under operational conditions most would have attempted to fly even lower. The well established low level navigation techniques, using timing marks and stopwatch, were successfully employed whether INAS was fitted or not. The most important facility offered by INAS in visual conditions was the ability to fly accurate track and groundspeed, while the continuous display of range and bearing to the target added tactical flexibility. If necessary, INAS present position could be updated although the track and groundspeed outputs would not be significantly improved. The most accurate method of updating was the 'Random Fix', although this could be pre-planned.

At night or in IMC conditions, navigation was dependent upon the INAS and radar or, in pre-INAS aircraft, upon radar alone. In aircraft not fitted with INAS the capability of the radar to provide navigation information was not a limiting factor upon penetration height because without any terrain following radar, IMC penetrations were not considered to be practicable below 500 ft AGL. In the early 1970s several NATO air forces began to use a navigation technique known as continuous mosaic radar prediction (CMRP) which, although not particularly flexible and involving a high workload, worked well enough. Radar prediction strips were produced for the required routes and a pattern-matching technique was then used to maintain track. A CMRP centre was soon operational at Bruggen and the technique was evaluated for use by Phantom and Buccaneer strike aircraft. Even with INAS fitted, frequent monitoring of position was required, together with the careful selection of waypoints to permit radar identification. However, conventional weapon delivery at the target was dependent on visual acquisition and aiming, so that for successful attacks it was essential that the target area be in visual conditions. Assuming adequate crew training it was concluded that the FGR.2 force would be capable of instrument penetrations in the height band 500–1,000 ft AGL over known terrain, given the limited penetration distances involved.

For the purposes of self defence, the Phantom was usually flown in the attack role with two Sparrow air-to-air missiles and the SUU 23 gun pod. The Sparrow was a semi-active radar missile which could be fired from low level provided that a radar lock had been achieved. The SUU 23 gun pod was primarily fitted for air-to-ground use but had been designed for air-to-air firing using a lead computing optical sighting system. The pod was difficult to maintain in harmonisation under conditions of high 'g' manoeuvring, but within its limitations it was a valuable air-to-air weapon. In the early days of Phantom operations in the RAF the level of crew training for gunnery was minimal, although this deficiency was soon addressed with increasingly frequent deployments to Akrotiri in Cyprus for Armament Practice Camps. As Sparrow missiles were not generally carried during routine training flights on 2ATAF squadrons, this meant that the aircraft/missile circuits were not under continual check. This, therefore gave rise to concern over the degree of technical reliability that would be achieved in a 'hot war' situation as the aircraft/missile circuits were not under continual check.

One of the first major modifications to the RAF Phantom fleet was the introduction of ARI 18228/1 passive warning radar. The system comprised three radar detection receivers covering frequencies in the 2.5–18 GHz range, a simple control unit and a Cathode Ray Tube (CRT) display unit located in the navigator's cockpit. The frequency bands of received signals were denoted by a visual coding system and the approximate relative bearing of each signal was given by the vector indicated on the CRT. Signals were also simultaneously converted into aural form, the pitch of which varied according to the Pulse Repetition Frequency (PRF), and relayed to the earphones of both pilot and navigator. With ARI 18228/1 installed the Phantom crew would be aware of the frequency band, scanning characteristics and approximate PRF and bearing of any radars illuminating the aircraft. With advance warning of a likely attack the crew would be able to take appropriate countermeasures to negate or minimise any threat before it reached dangerous proportions.

It was felt that any threat from enemy fighters to Phantom penetrations below 1,000 ft AGL was likely to be confined to visual conditions only. Intelligence sources indicated that Warsaw Pact fighters normally operated in pairs, the No. 2 flying a trail position 1,000–2,000 yards behind the leader during an attack. Their approach would normally be a visual descending curve so that even with passive warning radar equipment fitted to the FGR.2 there was unlikely to be a radar transmission to indicate the imminence of an attack. It was for this reason that it was essential for low level formations to keep a good lookout with each crew covering the other aircraft's blind spots.

Some benefit could also be obtained from the use of radar in air-to-air search during low level visual penetrations. Standard Operating Procedures (SOP) for Air Support Command squadrons at the time called for Nos. 1 and 3 in a four aircraft formation to be responsible for pulse Doppler in Auto Acquisition mode looking from level to 10 degrees up, with Nos. 2 and 4 using the radar in pulse from level to 10 degrees up. Although the use of the AWG-12 radar in pulse Doppler at heights of about 250 ft AGL was outside the equipment's design specification, there was evidence from the squadrons in RAF Germany that 'auto-acquisitions' were possible from this height on fighter type aircraft at ranges of 20–30 miles. Since the latest Intelligence assessment was that enemy fighters did not have passive warning receivers, other than tail warning, it was thought that the radar emissions produced by a penetrating formation would be of no aid to a fighter interception. Neither would there be any benefit to ground monitoring receivers which would have a limited range and, given the time scale under consideration, would not be able to act on any emissions that were picked up.

During low level penetrations, the aim, as far as possible, would be to avoid detection and engagement with defensive fighters in order to reach the target. The speed and manoeuvre limitations imposed by the weapons load would mean that, if engagement was unavoidable, all or part of the Phantom formation would have to jettison their attack loads in order to engage or outrun the enemy. This decision could only be made by the formation leader at the time in the light of the particular circumstances. Devoid of its load, a Phantom in full reheat, and at a low drag index, would have been able to outrun most Warsaw Pact fighters that it was likely to encounter in the early 1970s. It was estimated that the twin-engined Yak-25 Firebar had a maximum IAS at low level of 515 knots and the earlier MiG-21 Fishbed D and F models were limited to 595 knots. Even the latest version of the MiG-21, the Fishbed J, was thought to be only capable of 650 knots. Of course, in forcing the Phantom to jettison its weapons load the defending fighters would at least have achieved part of their aim.

It was felt that the carriage of air-to-air weapons would not affect the Phantom's ability to penetrate hostile airspace to any great extent, these mainly being an aid to survival if attacked. However, as the Phantom was only capable of making relatively short distance penetrations into East Germany it was possible that, if the conditions were right for a Sparrow missile engagement, any launch might be successful in either destroying the enemy or gaining sufficient time to reach the target.

The threat posed by surface to air missiles depended to a large extent on whether the attack was being carried out in visual or instrument/night conditions. In visual conditions at a penetration height of 250 ft AGL or below there was considered to be little likelihood of a successful SAM engagement, even allowing for the eventual deployment of SA-6 and the wider use of SA-3. When flying in night or instrument conditions in the height band between 500 and 1,000 ft any penetrating Phantom FGR.2s would be in the lower engagement envelope of most of the deployed SAM systems with the exception of the S-Band SA-2 which had a lower limit of 1,500 ft. The SA-4 was credited with a minimum engagement altitude limit of 1,000 ft, the C-Band SA-2 with 750 ft and the SA-3 with 500 ft. The SA-6 mobile system was also expected to have a lower limit of 500 ft. Until passive warning equipment was fitted, the only tactics available to Phantom crews were to avoid all known SAM sites and to remain below the minimum engagement altitudes when within enemy SAM cover.

The modification programme to install the radar warning receiver allowed crews of aircraft so fitted to be alerted to the presence of a threat by the sound of the SAM tracking radar detecting and acquiring its target. With appropriate training they would recognise the nature of the defensive system confronting them by the characteristic sound and frequency band of its associated radar. This warning period gave penetrating aircraft the opportunity to evade by reducing height (if possible), turning away from the threat and accelerating. The lack of any radar illumination also tended to reduce crew fatigue and allowed them to adapt their flight profile as necessary by flying at a slightly increased altitude to improve navigation and add to safety factors as regards terrain avoidance.

The third major element of Warsaw Pact defences was the formidable Anti-Aircraft Artillery (AAA). In visual conditions penetrating aircraft could be engaged by any of these weapons at any time, together with small arms fire. The most effective defensive measure in the face of this particular threat was to remain as low as possible. In instrument/night conditions, height and speed were still the major factors and since speed was limited by the need to conserve fuel, the requirement was to fly as low as possible. As the AAA computers ideally needed any target to fly in straight and level flight for accurate prediction, immediate avoiding action was to be taken should warning of an imminent engagement be received. Evasive action was the same as in the case of being attacked by a SAM battery, i.e. reduce height, accelerate and turn away from the threat.

In conclusion, CTTO considered that the main threat to Phantoms operating in the strike role in visual conditions over the north German plain would come from enemy fighters operating from Combat Air Patrols. Surface to air missiles could be virtually discounted altogether if attacking aircraft flew low enough, while the probability of random engagements by AAA would be small. In IMC or at night, fighters would not provide any significant opposition and the chances of attack from SAM sites or AAA were reduced the lower the attacking aircraft was able to fly. It was recommended that operational training concentrate on the following:

a) Overland visual navigation at 250 ft and below at 420 knots.
b) Overland radar navigation at 500 ft at 420 knots.
c) Low level handling, including fighter evasion.
d) Low level radar acquisition and simulated Sparrow engagements.
e) Missile firing practice and air-to-air gunnery training.
f) Recognition and reaction to audio warning of SAM and AAA fire control radars.

It was also recommended that the fitting of passive warning receiver ARI 18228/1 be treated as a matter of priority.

The Phantom FGR.2 continued in the strike, ground attack and tactical reconnaissance roles until the introduction of the SEPECAT Jaguar; the first unit to convert to the new aircraft being 54 Squadron which achieved operational status at Coltishall in August 1974. The Bruggen Wing survived a little longer but all three squadrons (Nos. 14, 17 and 31) had swapped their Phantoms for Jaguars by early 1976. Although the Jaguar had been specifically designed to fulfil the ground attack role and was better equipped to deal with low level turbulence thanks to its smaller wing, its lack of power when compared with the Phantom meant that the Phantom was sorely missed by the strike element of RAF Germany.

CHAPTER EIGHT

Phantom Tactics – Air Defence

After the decision not to equip a second Fleet Air Arm squadron with Phantoms for use aboard HMS *Eagle*, the RAF received a welcome boost with the delivery of twenty FG.1s previously allocated to the Royal Navy. These aircraft were taken on by 43 Squadron at Leuchars to fulfil the air defence role; the unit becoming fully operational in September 1969. With the Phantom set to take on air defence more fully from the mid 1970s, CTTO carried out a study of the Phantom in this role, the aim of which was to examine its combat potential compared with that of Eastern bloc fighter aircraft, and to determine suitable tactics. Although the examination centred on the Phantom FGR.2, the results obtained were equally applicable to the FG.1.

The tasking called for the formulation of tactics that would show how the Phantom could be manoeuvred to best advantage so as to achieve a kill, with emphasis being placed on seeking out and engaging the enemy, rather than self-defence. Fighter combat was considered in three separate phases. First, there was an opening phase which included the detection and identification of an opponent, followed by a development phase where the fighters manoeuvred for potential advantage and, finally, an end phase during which one fighter was able to achieve a firing opportunity. Certain assumptions were made in the compilation of the report as follows. Performance assessments were made on the basis that the Phantom and the Soviet fighters examined would be flown with half internal fuel, and that they would be equipped with maximum air-to-air missile armament but would otherwise be in clean configuration (mention was also made of other weapons loads, including podded guns). Ground control, or any other form of external assistance, was not available to the Phantom and it was assumed that ECM would not be used by either side.

In determining the capability of the Phantom in the air defence role, a close study had also to be made of the likely opposition. The Phantom would have had to contend with a wide variety of fighters ranging from the MiG-17 Fresco to the latest high performance, technologically advanced aircraft as represented by the Sukhoi Su-15 Flagon, MiG-23 Flogger and MiG-25 Foxbat. Such a diverse range of types meant that it was difficult to generalise about aircraft characteristics as each had its own advantages. Although it dated from the early 1950s, the Fresco could still be a difficult opponent with its exceptionally high rate of turn at low to medium altitudes, whilst the Flagon, Flogger and Foxbat had very high performance in terms of specific excess power. The majority of Soviet fighters had a high thrust-to-weight ratio, low wing-loading and possessed comparatively lightly constructed airframes with a small amount of internal fuel. Consequently these aircraft had excellent short range performance characteristics with excellent rates of climb and turn and a high ceiling, but they tended to suffer from severely restricted range, together with low maximum IAS and load factor limitations. A further disadvantage was that Soviet fighter aircraft tended to have limited cockpit visibility with rearward and upward vision restricted by the canopy design, plus a poor view forwards due to the thick bullet-proof windscreen.

When compared with the state of development in the West, Soviet fighter weapons systems were not as advanced and the level of sophistication of avionics in particular was poor. The radar systems used by even the latest fighters was inadequate for head-on missile attacks without fighter vectoring by an outside agency, and as their fire control systems and associated missiles were designed primarily for operation against non-evading targets, it was considered that Soviet fighters would be severely disadvantaged during fighter versus fighter combat.

Although the fighter tactics likely to be employed by Eastern bloc air forces were not fully known, enough information existed to indicate the basic philosophy of their operations. At the time that the CTTO report was compiled (1971) it appeared that Soviet fighter aircraft did not have any air superiority role, but rather operated in the interceptor and ground attack roles. Great reliance was placed on ground radars to provide close control of the interceptor via data-link, thus compensating for the lack of advanced systems in the aircraft itself. Under this form of control, particular emphasis was placed on the importance of surprise: the fighter flying a ‘silent approach’ under data-link guidance, only switching on its AI radar when in a position to attain lock-on and an early missile launch. Warsaw Pact forces had recently taken on the concept of CAP against low level targets but even so, close control was still preferred, reverting to visual search only as a last resort. Because of the problems of obtaining radar lock, the final attack on low level targets was invariably visual, running in from about 2 nm at a closing speed of 50–100 knots at 15–45 degrees off the tail.

The general assessment of Soviet operating philosophy was that air combat was not seen as being particularly important and little training was carried out in this aspect of operations. Because of the heavy reliance on ground control, individual initiative was not encouraged, and it was felt by CTTO that if instructions from the ground could be denied by electronic means then the combat effectiveness of threat aircraft would be degraded even further, as neither aircraft nor training at that time was orientated towards autonomous operations.

In comparison with most Soviet fighters, the advantages enjoyed by Phantom crews were longer range, greater power (especially at low to medium altitudes) and a significantly better weapons system. The Phantom had been designed and optimised for long-range front hemisphere missile attacks against non-evading targets, but over the years it had been constantly updated, in particular the development of the dogfight mode of the Sparrow missile, to improve its capability in air combat. The AWG-11/12 was one of the best airborne radars of its day and in pulse Doppler mode it was capable of detecting a target of MiG-25 Foxbat size at 39 nm with an 85 per cent reliability rate. Should such a target be flying at co-altitude or higher, a range of around 47 nm could be expected.

Trials results with earlier Phantom aircraft using pulse mode had showed that detection ranges in this case were somewhat less. Given knowledge that an attack was imminent, together with information relating to height and range, a Phantom size target could be detected at a range of 25 nm, provided it was at or above the fighter's altitude. When this information was not available however, and a true 'unknown' threat was simulated, the mean detection range dropped to 13–14 nm. Targets flying below the fighters were rarely detected using pulse mode. The chances of locating target aircraft in pulse were improved with a flight of four aircraft, detection rates of at least 80 per cent being achieved, although there was little effect as regards range. The effectiveness of the AWG-11/12 radar was also governed by the height at which operations were carried out. The Phantom's radar search capability began to be reduced below 4,000 ft with side lobe returns starting to swamp the radar receiver. Below 1,000 ft, interference between the main beam clutter and side lobe returns produced 'birdies' in pulse Doppler, with much degraded performance in manual search and false locks in auto-acquisition mode.

In pulse mode the search capability was also reduced, even against high flying targets (subsequent modifications did improve this situation).

At the time it was released to service, the launch limitation for the Sparrow missile was relatively low at +2 or +3 g depending on the particular station being used. This imposed considerable operating restrictions in the fighter role which, of necessity, required high-g loadings in order to attain a firing position. Trials carried out by the US Navy recommended Sparrow be cleared for firing up to aircraft limiting 'g', but for a time the Phantom's combat effectiveness was considerably reduced. Problems were also experienced with CW (continuous wave) radar interference which could cause the Sparrow missile to fuse prematurely. This could occur if two or more Phantoms were operating on the same CW illuminator frequency and it became an important factor in formation planning.

In the near-miss, high closing-speed situation, which was likely to occur on a head-on missile launch, difficulty was also experienced with correct fusing of the AIM 7E-2. The incidence of premature fusing depended on the characteristics of the target and was particularly affected by the compressor or turbine modulation returns exhibited by many Soviet fighter aircraft. In these circumstances it appeared that Sparrow had a very low lethality rate, with a single-shot kill probability against a MiG-21 Fishbed of only 0.39 if fusing occurred on modulation returns. The Sparrow missile was also prone to premature fusing in a look-down, shoot-down situation and for low level targets over land (or over rough seas) lethality was very low. In these cases, the best results were to be obtained by making a near head-on attack using pulse Doppler radar, aiming for a 5–8 degree look-down angle and launching the missile within 4 nm range.

The other main element of the Phantom weapons system was the AIM-9D Sidewinder heat seeking missile. The first successful test firing of the Sidewinder had taken place as long ago as September 1953 but it had been the subject of constant upgrades and by the early 1970s the -9D was still one of the most effective weapons in air combat once a fighter had managed to manoeuvre into a suitable position in the rear hemisphere of its target. Within the launch envelope of the missile, and provided that a good audio infra-red (IR) return had been obtained, the AIM-9D could be used for an immediate opportunity shot, however, there were several factors that had to be taken into consideration to ensure its effectiveness.

Coolant was provided for at least two hours of continuous operation of the missile system although it took around one minute to cool the seeker to operating temperature after activation. It was important therefore to select coolant prior to entering the combat zone. The supply was self-regulating, and no saving of coolant was made by switching the system off for short periods. Missile guidance could be severely degraded by interference from a background of cloud, ground or even the moon, and the aircraft had to be flown to a position where the target IR could be distinguished from background emissions. As an example, target IR discrimination was almost doubled if the target was silhouetted against a blue sky rather than cloud or the ground. Against a target using reheat, the missile was also liable to lock on to the hottest portion of the reheat plume which was often sufficiently far enough behind the target to cause a significant reduction in lethality. Whenever possible, attacks were best made from below but not within 30 degrees of the sun. Unlike the Sparrow, the Sidewinder could not be ripple fired since the second missile would home on to the IR emission of the first.

Carriage of the SUU-23 gun pod imposed penalties in terms of aircraft performance, together with operational limitations. Internal guns as fitted to the F-4E had been used with great success in air combat in south-east Asia and the Middle East, however, any decision to carry the gun pod on RAF Phantoms needed careful consideration. The main operational limitations of the SUU-23 gun pod were as follows:

a) A one second gunsight tracking time required to produce lead computation.
b) Inaccuracy of the sight computation.
c) A gun reaction time of 0.4 sec to build up to a full rate of fire.
d) Loss of gun pod harmonisation particularly during high-g manoeuvring.

Any study of air fighting, even from the very earliest days, would show that the majority of kills were achieved against aircraft that had not detected the presence of a hostile fighter. In the formulation of suitable tactics for the Phantom, nothing had changed and it was imperative that opposing fighters be denied the opportunity of approaching to a weapon launch position. To achieve this it was necessary to make full use of the active radar and passive ECM receiver, with visual detection as a backup.

To get the most out of the AWG-11/12 radar the Phantom should be operated above 4,000 ft AGL and should use pulse Doppler (PD) and look-down search to detect low level targets. Because of the narrow radar beam in single-bar search and the relatively poor antenna elevation display of the radar, the search pattern had to be accurately set up if gaps in the radar cover were to be avoided. Search patterns and radar modes had to be allocated between formation members and these patterns had to be maintained to achieve complete radar cover from ground level upwards. Generally the best results would be obtained from the PD mode and multibar scan.

A practical search method for a formation of four aircraft would be for the navigators of the lead aircraft to concentrate their efforts on radar search, while those in the wing aircraft would devote their time to lookout but, at the same time, backing up the radar search by operating their radars in PD auto-acquisition. There was, however, a danger in PD mode that the wingmen would lock onto the turbine modulation returns from the lead aircraft, particularly if the formation adopted was too swept. To guard against targets crossing at shallow angles, which could go undetected by PD radar, it was recommended that one of the lead aircraft should operate in pulse mode. For a two aircraft formation, it was best for both aircraft to operate in PD auto-acquisition which would allow the navigators to contribute to the visual search, and by switching one or other of the aircraft's radars to pulse from time to time, the possibility of shallow crossing angle targets escaping detection would be reduced.

Although any war scenario in northern Europe was likely to lead to a highly complex radar picture, the selective use of passive warning radar was a useful asset to alert crews to the fact that they had been illuminated by a high data-rate (locked on) AI radar. Even allowing for the 'silent approach' technique of Soviet fighters, where the AI radar was only switched on immediately before lock-on, the Passive Warning Receiver (PWR) was still invaluable for indicating the presence of a previously undetected imminent threat.

Irrespective of the efficiency of radar search, the maximum cover obtainable was only 120 degrees so that a visual search had to be executed to obtain cover through a full 360 degrees. Visual detection ranges depended on many factors such as size and altitude of the target, contrast, terrain, cloud reflections, smoke emission etc, but assuming conditions of bright sunlight, a high contrast between target and background and with the pilot looking directly at the target aircraft, a MiG-21 size aircraft could normally be seen at around 7 nm. However, as the pilot would normally be engaged in a systematic search of all areas, a more realistic figure was 3 nm. Trials carried out in the USA indicated that a J79-engined Phantom was normally detected at around 6.5 nm, this figure increasing to 12 nm when head-on or tail-on due to its smoke trail.

Target identification posed a problem in a non-GCI environment as in most cases weapon release could only be made following a visual identification. Trials showed that the identity of a target was only confirmed at relatively short ranges of 1–2 nm when operating in day, Visual Meteorological Conditions (VMC) and against other fighters.

With a visident [visual identification], the Sparrow and Sidewinder firing envelopes were such that the only form of attack available was from the rear, so that the head-on capability of the Phantom could only be exploited using a pair of aircraft, one to identify and the other to attack. The only alternative was to train crews to recognise individual radar types via the PWR.

In any air combat situation it is vitally important for a pilot to maintain the initiative. Having located a threat, the opening phase of combat was characterised by the need to increase the manoeuvre potential of the fighter by increasing its energy level. If a climb was required, the initial acceleration was best performed by unloading the Phantom to 5–7 units AOA, and to avoid excessive loss of energy when intercepting the desired climb path, no more than 3–4 g was to be applied at subsonic speeds, with not more than 2 g when supersonic.

Having attained an adequate energy level by accelerating and/or climbing, the aim was then to obtain positional advantage without sacrificing any of this advantage and, consequently, losing the potential for effective manoeuvring. The objective at all times was to operate the Phantom in areas in which it was superior to its adversary, both in terms of aircraft performance and in its weapons system. Generally this involved avoiding a turning fight whenever possible and concentrating on keeping energy levels high by using vertical manoeuvres. Rates of turn had to be restricted so that there was no loss of energy relative to the opponent.

Moving into the end phase of an air combat, unless multiple targets constituted a continued threat, the need to maintain a high energy level was less important once the Phantom had manoeuvred into a firing position. Pilot technique became of critical importance at this stage. For example, the lift characteristics of the Phantom were such that there was no increase in lift between 20 and 22 units AOA, but there was a considerable rise in drag. Although increased lift and, hence, increased rate of turn, was obtained above 24 units AOA, drag was very high and longitudinal stability deteriorated rapidly. As a general rule, unless it was intended to dissipate energy to obtain a shot, the maximum recommended was about 20 units AOA.

The Phantom's major deficiency in terms of performance was its poor rate of turn, its 'g' capability for the same height and speed being inferior to the majority of Soviet fighters. This led to the development of a leading edge slat first fitted to the USAF F-4E which improved the aircraft's turn capability and allowed an extra ¼–1 g to be pulled throughout most of the flight envelope and greatly improved handling qualities at high AOA. Additionally, the slat allowed deletion of the BLC system which improved aircraft survivability and servicing.

One significant advantage that the Phantom did possess when compared with Eastern bloc opposition was the superiority of the Sparrow missile. Most Soviet air-to-air missiles of the early 1970s did not have a good capability against manoeuvring targets, and in the front hemisphere were restricted to a narrow head-on sector. Sparrow could be used outside this zone and it provided the Phantom with an exclusive firing area relative to all Soviet aircraft, although this advantage was likely to be reduced if visual identification was required. Having achieved a firing position it was recommended that a pair of Sparrow missiles be ripple-fired. When in the rear hemisphere of a target the Sidewinder became the primary weapon due to its faster reaction time, shorter tracking time, snapshot firing capability, higher launch 'g' tolerance and a higher single-shot kill probability.

The size and structure of Phantom tactical formations depended very much on the type of mission being flown. In any conflict RAF Phantoms were likely to be outnumbered so that it was essential that individual aircraft be employed as efficiently as possible. During counter air missions, the basic four aircraft battle formation provided the optimum detection capability, at the same time as allowing effective visual search and mutual support. Normal spacing of the formation was 2 nm with altitude being determined by factors such as weather, the likely enemy threat and the location of the probable combat area. Once combat had been joined the formation would generally split into two pairs, the tactics available to each pair depending on the number and aggressiveness of the enemy aircraft and the level of advantage held by either adversary after the initial contact phase. As already stated, it was best to avoid a close-quarters turning fight at all costs and instead strive for a disengaged form of combat in which only one Phantom was committed at a time, the other aircraft staying in visual contact with the fight and maintaining its energy level.

An analysis of air combat over the years also shows that one of the most dangerous periods is the disengagement. Owing to the need to maintain high energy levels, the Phantom had to be flown in reheat for much of the time and high rates of fuel consumption could result in an early exit from the fight. So as not to expose itself unduly, the Phantom had to take advantage of the Soviet fighter's relatively low IAS limitation and poor weapon capability against low level targets by escaping at high speed and very low level. The recommended fuel limit was 4,000 lb which allowed five minutes combat at low level with selective use of reheat. The timing of the escape manoeuvre was critical and, if possible, was to be executed when the opponent was unable to follow. Use of reheat was to be kept to a minimum to decrease the chances of the Phantom being acquired by an IR missile and a turn into sun would also reduce the effectiveness of Soviet missiles during this vulnerable phase of combat.

In the final part of its report, CTTO compared the Phantom with the MiG-21, its principal rival in Vietnam. At the time the older Fishbed D/F was still the most numerous MiG-21 variant in service with Warsaw Pact air forces. Its weapons system was vastly inferior to that of the Phantom as its Spin Scan B radar had search and track ranges of only 10.8 and 8.1 nm respectively, requiring accurate close control in order to attain a position in the rear hemisphere of a target for missile launch. The restricted lock-on envelope of the system also required accurate tracking at a fairly early stage of engagement. In addition, the Spin Scan B radar was not stabilised which meant that it would have been very difficult to obtain a radar lock against an evading target. Even when using a look-up technique, side lobe returns would degrade radar performance to a maximum of around 3 nm at lower levels. Hence in a non-GCI environment the Phantom would enjoy considerable advantage, although this would be reduced if operations were being carried out in an area where close ground control was available to the MiG.

The Phantom also had the advantage of better and more varied weapons than the MiG-21F. In the all-weather role the latter was still likely to be equipped with the old 'Alkali' radar-guided missile which, like the infra-red 'Atoll', could not be launched in a high-g turn. It also had no head-on capability and could only be launched within a 20 degree cone to the rear of the target with the wings of the launch aircraft within 15 degrees of level. Furthermore, 'Alkali' required radar lock to be maintained throughout its flight. Even if a MiG-21F was detected in an attacking position, provided that the Phantom kept speed and 'g' high, the missile capability of the MiG was severely restricted.

The Phantom also possessed a significant advantage in terms of aircraft performance especially at low to medium altitudes at speeds up to 1.4 M. The area of superiority of the MiG was confined essentially to high speeds at medium to high altitudes. In addition, the Phantom had a large exclusive area where the MiG was unable to operate because of its lower IAS limit. Phantom crews also had the luxury of being able to increase energy levels more rapidly than the MiG for any start condition below 1.6 M. This advantage was continued into the development phase of air combat, the Phantom having better specific excess power for flight at high 'g' levels. Due to the MiG's handling restrictions and small amount of internal fuel, the Phantom was at its best at high IAS at low level where it had at least 400 ft/sec advantage over its opponent.

In the final stage of combat where the Phantom was approaching a firing position, rate of turn became the most significant factor. Comparative turn plots showed that the Phantom had the advantage provided speed was kept high above 0.6 M at sea level or 1.1 M at 30,000 ft. However, if speed was allowed to drop, the combat rapidly entered an area of overwhelming MiG superiority. In this case an examination of the Phantom's specific excess power showed a large negative value. Although the MiG was also losing speed at this point, the reduction in energy level was not occurring as quickly as with the Phantom. As a result, maximum rate turn performance had only to be used by the Phantom when its pilot was absolutely certain that he would attain a kill position. Another aspect of the performance of the British Phantom was that the Spey engine, being a turbofan with a very high mass flow rate, was much more sensitive to temperature alterations than the straight turbojets of Soviet fighters. Consequently, on any given day, performance could be much different from that quoted in the Flight Manual.

Although the Phantom's performance against the MiG-21D/F may have been significantly better, this variant was already ten years old and was being supplanted by the much improved Fishbed H/J. Despite the fact that the Phantom still had the edge in having the ability to launch front hemisphere attacks, the new MiG was fitted with 'Jaybird' radar and semi-active 'Atoll' air-to-air missiles which provided much greater flexibility and all-weather capability. A built-in gun was an effective short range weapon and was of particular use when it came to close-in combat at high 'g'.

Improvements to the MiG's IAS and 'g' limitations considerably reduced the Phantom's exclusive zone and its superiority was further reduced as the new variant was powered by an R-13 turbojet which produced approximately 20 per cent more thrust in reheat than the previous Tumansky-designed R-11. Thus in the opening phase of any engagement the area of Phantom superiority was limited to virtually subsonic flight. Above 1.3 M the MiG had superiority at any altitude and the Phantom exclusive area had virtually disappeared. In the development stage of combat, particularly if 'g' loads were kept high, the Phantom still enjoyed considerable advantage as the increased drag and weight of the MiG tended to balance out its extra power.

Assuming that the Phantom was able to dictate the terms of any fight, it had nothing to fear from the MiG-21 but by the early 1970s the Soviet Air Force was introducing several new types such as the Sukhoi Su-15 Flagon and MiG-23. Clearly if the Phantom was to maintain any level of superiority against these more advanced fighters it would have to be continually updated. Areas of concern as identified by CTTO were the Phantom weapons system, particularly the poor reaction time of Sparrow which severely inhibited operations in the front hemisphere and the lack of a built-in gun. It was also hoped that consideration would be given to procuring the Sidewinder Expanded Acquisition Mode (SEAM) and the possibility of fitting leading edge slats to provide an improvement in turn performance. The Phantom weapon system was gradually upgraded over the years, the standard weapons fit eventually comprising the all-aspect AIM-9L Sidewinder and the BAe Dynamics Sky Flash, a major redesign of the AIM-7E2.

CHAPTER NINE

F-4J Handling Characteristics

When the development of the Panavia Tornado air defence variant ran into problems, and with the Lightning about to be retired, the RAF was left with the prospect of having a distinct fighter shortage in the mid to late 1980s. This short term requirement was addressed by the purchase of fifteen refurbished ex-US Navy F-4J Phantoms which had been languishing at the storage depot at Davis Monthan AFB in the Arizona desert. These were delivered to the UK towards the end of 1984 to be flown by 74 'Tiger' Squadron which was re-formed at Wattisham. Wherever possible the F-4J (UK) had been modified to be compatible with aircraft already in service including wiring for Sky Flash missiles and the SUU-23 gun pod. The radar was brought up to AN/AWG-10B digital standard and the AN/ALR-45 radar warning receiver was replaced with ALR-66. Although most aircraft had plenty of flying hours left in them, the F-4J (UK) was eventually withdrawn from use in January 1991 as a result of spares shortages and rising maintenance costs. The J was powered by General Electric J79-GE-10B engines with quicker reheat response and better altitude performance than the Spey powered Phantom and was well liked by those who flew it. The following is a description of its handling characteristics taken from the US Navy's NATOPS Flight Manual as issued to 74 Squadron crews.

LOW ANGLE OF ATTACK MANOEUVRING

Induced drag is at a minimum at approximately 5 units AOA (nearly zero 'g'); therefore, acceleration characteristics are exceptional. To achieve maximum performance acceleration from subsonic Mach numbers to supersonic flight, a 5 unit AOA pushover will provide minimum drag and allow gravity to enhance aeroplane acceleration. This technique provides the minimum time, fuel and distance to accelerate from subsonic Mach numbers to the optimum supersonic climb schedule. When confronted with a recovery from a condition of low airspeed and high pitch attitude, the AOA indicator becomes the primary recovery instrument. A smooth pushover to 5 units AOA will unload the aeroplane and reduce the stall speed to nearly zero. Recovery can be accomplished safely at any speed which will provide stabilator effectiveness. Smooth control of AOA is a necessity and no attempt to control bank angle or yaw should be made. High pitch angles with rapidly decreasing airspeed will result in loss of stabilator effectiveness and subsequent loss of control of AOA.

Medium Angle of Attack Manoeuvring

Manoeuvring at angles of attack from 5 to 15 units will produce normal aeroplane response to control movements.

High Angle of Attack Manoeuvring

Above 15 units AOA, aeroplane response and flight characteristics begin to exhibit the changes expected of swept-wing high performance aircraft. The primary flight characteristics exhibited at high angles of attack are adverse yaw (yaw due to roll) and dihedral effect (roll due to yaw).

Adverse Yaw

Attempts to roll the aeroplane with lateral stick deflections (ailerons and spoilers) will result in yaw opposite to the direction of the intended turn. This adverse yaw becomes more severe at high angles of attack. In the high AOA flight regime, aileron inputs provide very low roll rates. At very high angles of attack (near stall), aileron inputs cause increased adverse yaw and roll opposite to that intended. The natural tendency to raise the wing with aileron must be avoided. Aileron deflection at the point of departure from controlled flight will increase the probability of spin entry. At the first indication of adverse yaw, the ailerons must be neutralised. (Note – With 'roll stab aug' engaged, roll rates not commanded by lateral stick deflection will cause aileron deflection against the roll. At high angles of attack this will cause pro-spin adverse yaw in opposition to rudder induced roll and will increase the probability of departure from controlled flight. 'Roll aug' should be selected OFF for air combat manoeuvring.)

DIHEDRAL EFFECT

Attempts to yaw the aeroplane with rudder will produce roll in the same direction as yaw. This dihedral effect becomes more pronounced at high angles of attack. The use of rudder inputs to produce yaw and in turn generate roll, will provide the highest attainable roll rates at high angles of attack. Above 15 units AOA, desired roll should be generated primarily through use of the rudder. The rudder must be used judiciously, however, since excessive rudder inputs will induce excessive yaw.

LANDING

The optimum approach (ON SPEED) indicated AOA with the landing gear down is 19.0 units, and stall warning (rudder pedal shaker) is set to 21.3 units. The AOA reference changes with nose gear position in the approach speed range. The indicated AOA increases approximately 3 units when the nose gear is extended. This is due to a change in the airflow pattern over the fuselage mounted AOA probe with the nose gear retracted. All references to indicated AOA should take this factor into consideration. Optimum approach AOA is adequate for all allowable gross weight and flap configurations. No adjustment is required for gusting crosswinds, runway or weather conditions.

MINIMUM PERFORMANCE MANOEUVRING

Manoeuvrability and handling qualities are degraded at lower airspeeds with sluggish response and low available 'g'; therefore, maintain a minimum 300 knots except during maximum range descent, holding, instrument approach and landing. This airspeed provides reasonable handling qualities and adequate manoeuvre margin for terrain and collision avoidance.

MAXIMUM PERFORMANCE MANOEUVRING

The three factors that determine maximum performance manoeuvring capability are structural limitations, stabilator effectiveness and aerodynamic limitations. The limit in stabilator effectiveness occurs at high altitudes and supersonic speeds where full aft stick can be attained without reaching aerodynamic or structural limits. Aerodynamic limitations (stall) are primarily a function of AOA. In this area of flight, maximum performance turns are achieved by maintaining 19 to 20 units AOA while utilising afterburner as required. The adverse yaw produced by the use of ailerons during high AOA maximum performance manoeuvring has been discussed and is of paramount importance in Air Combat Manoeuvring. If a high AOA must be maintained and a roll is necessary, rudder must be used to produce roll due to yaw as previously discussed. During maximum performance manoeuvring, higher roll rates may be achieved by momentarily unloading the aeroplane (reducing AOA to between 5 and 10 units), utilising aileron to roll to the desired bank angle, then neutralising aileron and re-establishing the required AOA. At the first indication of departure from controlled flight, controls must be neutralised to preclude aggravating the out-of-control condition.

HANDLING QUALITIES – SUBSONIC REGION

TAKE OFF CONFIGURATION

Take-off performance is based on aeroplane gross weight and CG position. Lift-off speed is a function of gross weight and is essentially the speed at which the wings develop sufficient lift to raise the weight of the aeroplane. Nosewheel lift-off is a function of CG, stabilator position and gross weight. Nosewheel lift-off occurs when the nose-up aerodynamic moment exceeds the nose-down weight moment. The stabilator cannot be stalled in the take-off manoeuvre. Therefore, full aft stick take-off technique (full leading edge down stabilator) provides the lowest nosewheel lift-off speed and the shortest take-off distance. For full aft stick, the CG position will determine when the rotation begins; a lower speed than lift-off with an aft CG, and a higher speed than lift-off with a forward CG. The rate of rotation is a function of aeroplane acceleration (rate of build up of down tail lift) and CG. Therefore, because of the rapid build up of pitch-rate at aft CG, full aft or rapid stick displacements can cause over-rotation following the nosewheel lift-off phase. In computing CG for take-off, allowance must be made for the forward shift of CG during ground operation. The CG will move forward approximately 1 per cent for every 1,000 lb of internal fuel used. In the forward CG range, nosewheel lift-off speed is increased approximately 4–5 knots for every per cent of forward CG movement. After nosewheel lift-off, desired pitch attitude is maintained by using whatever control movement is required.

LANDING CONFIGURATION

In this configuration, the aeroplane exhibits positive longitudinal static stability except for an area about 10 knots before the stall where a mild stick force lightening occurs. This is followed by a regaining of static stability after the stall so that if back pressure is released, the aeroplane recovers by itself. In the speed range 130–180 knots, where most landing configuration flying is done, the aeroplane demonstrates almost neutral stick force stability up to about 150 knots and mild stick force stability above this speed. This is due to control system friction and rather weak stick centring at this low Q. Stabilator effectiveness is reduced with full flaps due to an aft centre of pressure shift and a change in the down wash pattern over the tail. However, adequate effectiveness still remains for all known configurations. Since ground effect also decreases stabilator effectiveness, the aft stick-stop may be bumped during flare out from a high sink rate landing. Stabilator effectiveness is not sufficient to hold the nose up after landing since the centre of rotation is now about the main gear instead of the CG.

Lateral and directional control response in the landing configuration is good; however, adverse yaw generated by high roll rates produces a decrease in commanded roll due to strong dihedral effect. This strong dihedral effect can be utilised in the landing configuration to provide roll with rudder deflection. Judicious use of rudder at approach angles of attack can provide desired roll response. The ARI (Aileron-Rudder Interconnect) feeds in rudder automatically to counteract yaw so that when large amounts of aileron are being used, the turn will be co-ordinated. Except for unusually asymmetrical external loadings or very rough, gusty air, only small lateral control motions are required for landing. The approach to the stall is characterised by a decrease in lateral stability which becomes evident by a mild wing-rock (5–10 degrees) which gets progressively worse as speed is reduced.

CLEAN CONFIGURATION

Lateral and directional control response is good in the clean configuration and the aeroplane exhibits good pilot feel. Rate of roll is quite high in this area and directional stability is strong enough so that ball-centred turns are made without the use of rudder. During abrupt aileron rolls, where some adverse yaw is experienced, the yaw damper is effective in keeping the ball centred.

TRANSONIC REGION

HIGH ALTITUDE

In the transonic region, longitudinal static stability becomes more positive and stabilator effectiveness somewhat reduced resulting in a slightly higher stick force gradient. The transition from transonic to subsonic speeds while holding G on the aeroplane results in a mild to moderate nose rise. If corrective action is not taken, this could place the aeroplane in buffet at higher altitudes or cause a significant load factor increase at lower altitudes. This is characteristic of most swept-wing aeroplanes and is a result of going from an area of higher stability and lower stabilator effectiveness to an area of lower static stability and higher stabilator effectiveness. Speed brakes increase the nose rise tendency during transition from transonic to subsonic speeds. Lateral and directional control in the transonic region is about the same as that experienced in the subsonic region, except that roll rate capability is higher. Roll rates are highest in the transonic region; however, in both transonic and subsonic regions, roll rate resulting from full aileron is much too great for any practical use.

LOW ALTITUDE

Transonic flight at low altitude presents a low stick force gradient and high stabilator effectiveness which results in an area of high sensitivity and possible over-control. Even though the inherent dynamic stability of the aeroplane is positive, it may be possible to create a short period longitudinal oscillation if the pilot's response becomes out of phase with the aeroplane motion, thereby inducing negative damping. Such a condition is commonly known as a pilot induced oscillation (PIO). Since the dampers will decrease the stabilator response to rapid stick inputs, the possibility of inducing PIO is minimised with dampers on. It is recommended that the stability augmentation be used when flying at high speeds and low altitudes.

The standard and most effective recovery technique from a PIO is to release the controls. An out-of-trim condition is conducive to PIO, and releasing controls while stick forces are present, because of an out-of-trim condition, could amplify the oscillation. Therefore, it becomes advisable to trim out longitudinal stick forces during rapid afterburner acceleration at low altitudes. It should be noted, however, that if longitudinal trim forces are trimmed out while manoeuvring, an out-of-trim condition will be present when returning to wings-level flight necessitating a push force to hold altitude. If the altitude of a mission is such that it would not be desirable to release the flight controls, recovery from a PIO can be accomplished by making the arm and body as rigid as possible, even bracing the left hand against the canopy and either holding the stick in the approximate trim position or by applying slight positive g-loading. In addition, afterburner shutdown at high IAS can produce a pitch transient.

Abrupt pitch inputs could cause an oscillation to begin; therefore, all corrections should be performed smoothly. Always lock the shoulder straps when flying under conditions of high speed and low altitude. The body, from the lap belt up, could become the forcing function during an inadvertent pitch input if the shoulder straps are unlocked.

SUPERSONIC REGION

HIGH ALTITUDE

Longitudinal static stability gets more positive as Mach number is increased in the supersonic region. Stabilator effectiveness decreases somewhat, so manoeuvring stick forces become higher but do not exceed 10–12 lb per 'g'. Manoeuvring capability is limited by stabilator effectiveness at the higher Mach numbers at higher altitudes; for example, full aft stick at Mach 2 at 50,000 ft will produce about 3.5 G. No abnormal lateral or directional control problems exist during supersonic flight. Directional stability remains strong and rate of roll, although decreasing with Mach number, remains quite adequate out to limit Mach numbers.

ZOOM CLIMBS

A zoom climb can be performed by accelerating to a high energy condition and then slowly rotating to a pitch attitude higher than normal climb. Pitch attitudes in excess of 60 degrees detract from zoom climb capability and produce more uncomfortable recovery conditions. During a zoom climb to altitudes above 65,000 ft, the EGT must be monitored. Afterburner blow-out will usually occur at around 67,000 to 70,000 ft. When the afterburners blow out, the throttles should be taken out of the afterburner range to preclude unexpected or hard lightoffs during descent. Above 70,000 ft the engines will have to be shut down if they tend to overspeed or over-temp. Engine windmill speed at altitudes above 70,000 ft is high enough to maintain some cockpit pressurisation and normal electrical power. Stabilator effectiveness will decrease noticeably above 50,000 ft and an increased amount of aft stick will be required to hold a given pitch attitude.

Zoom climb recovery can be initiated at any time during the manoeuvre by relaxing back pressure on the stick and flying the aeroplane over the top at a 'g' loading which will prevent stall. Maintaining a constant value of AOA between 5 and 10 units will properly decrease 'g' with decreasing airspeed during the recovery while still maintaining a safe positive 'g' loading on the aircraft. Negative 'g' recoveries are not recommended because of aircraft and physiological limitations and lack of pilot ability to detect impending stall. Two basic methods of recovering from the zoom climb are possible. A wings-level recovery can be effected by smoothly decreasing AOA to the minimum positive 'g' value and holding this until the aeroplane is diving. An inverted recovery can be effected by controlling AOA while rolling the aeroplane to inverted and then increasing AOA to produce the maximum 'g' loading on the aeroplane.

A comparison of the two techniques shows that the positive 'g' loading on the aeroplane assists the recovery trajectory in the inverted case whereas it detracts from the recovery trajectory in the wings-level case. The resulting flatter trajectory of the wings-level recovery produces a lower minimum airspeed and higher maximum altitude over the top in addition to a longer overall recovery time. Although the inverted recovery is superior from the standpoint of speed, altitude and exposure time, it exhibits certain risks due to pilot capabilities to properly control AOA during the rolling manoeuvres. All zoom climb recoveries demand smooth co-ordinated control action. The AOA indication is the primary recovery aid regardless of method. As speed decreases, the stabilator required to develop a given pitch command increases. Higher than normal stick displacements and rates will be necessary to command or hold AOA at very low speeds. Inadvertent pitch inputs due to abrupt roll action or pilot's inattention to required pitch control can quickly put the aeroplane in a stalled condition.

Zoom climb recoveries initiated from indicated airspeeds in excess of 250 knots can be made inverted or wings-level. For the wings-level recovery, smoothly reduce AOA to 5 units and hold this value until the aeroplane is in a recovery dive, and speed has increased through 250 knots. Attempts to hasten the recovery by pushing over to a value below 5 units AOA will produce negative 'g' and a possible stall. Precise roll attitude is not important during the recovery. Any aileron used to correct or maintain roll attitude should be smooth and co-ordinated. For the inverted recovery, smoothly reduce AOA to 5 units and holding this value, smoothly roll the aeroplane to inverted. Increase and hold AOA at 10 units to produce maximum safe 'g' loading on the aeroplane. When in an inverted recovery dive, the roll to wings-level must again be accomplished with smooth slow control action while holding AOA between 5–10 units. As before, AOA should be maintained in the recovery dive until airspeed builds up to 250 knots.

Zoom climb recoveries initiated at airspeeds less than 250 knots should be accomplished with pilot's sole attention devoted to proper control of AOA between 5–10 units. Roll attitude should be completely ignored with aileron and rudder held generally neutral to maintain co-ordinated flight. If a pilot becomes confused or disorientated during any recovery, he should immediately concentrate only on AOA and ignore all other parameters. If AOA is maintained between 5–10 units, the aeroplane will recover safely to a nose-down accelerating condition, regardless of roll attitude.

STALLS – CRUISE/COMBAT CONFIGURATION

NORMAL STALLS

Normal (1'g') stalls are preceded by a wide band of buffet. First noticeable buffet occurs at 12 to 14 units AOA and usually increases from moderate to heavy buffet immediately prior to stall or departure. The rudder pedal shaker is activated at 21.3 units, however, it may not be recognisable due to heavy buffet. Wing rock, if encountered, will commence at approximately 23 units and variations in bank angle of up to 30 degrees from wings level can be expected near the stall. The angle of attack at stall varies with loading and is normally above 25 units. The stall is characterised by a slight nose rise and/or yawing motion in either direction. Recovery from the stall is easily and immediately effected when AOA is reduced by positioning the stick forward, maintaining neutral ailerons and making judicious use of rudder to avoid inducing excessive yaw.

ACCELERATED STALLS

Specific characteristics vary with airspeed, Mach number, loading, CG, 'g' level, aeroplane attitude and control technique. In general accelerated stalls are preceded by moderate buffet which increases to heavy buffet immediately prior to the stall. Wing rock is unpredictable, but generally starts at about 22 to 25 units and progresses to a high frequency, large amplitude roll oscillation. The amplitude of the roll oscillations will be less with a heavy wing loaded aeroplane. AOA at stall varies considerably with loading, but is above 25 units for all loadings. Rapidly entered accelerated stalls may occur at lower indicated angles of attack. Increasing the rate of aft stick displacement increases the magnitude and rate of yaw and roll oscillations at the stall. Applying and holding full aft stick, even with ailerons and rudder neutral, can result in a spin. Prompt neutralisation of controls will effect recovery from an accelerated stall. Oscillations in roll and yaw, which may be present during recovery should be allowed to damp themselves out and should not be countered with ailerons or rudder.

INVERTED STALLS

An inverted (negative angle of attack) stall can only be obtained with abrupt application of full forward stick in vertical manoeuvres or an inverted climb of greater than 20 degrees nose up. Light to moderate buffet occurs at the stall and there are no distinct yaw or roll tendencies. Recovery from the inverted stall is effected by relaxing the forward stick pressure and maintaining an angle of attack between 5 and 10 units until recovered from the unusual attitude.

LOSS OF CONTROL

A loss of control or departure from controlled flight is best described as random motions about any or all axes. Departure characteristics are highly dependent on airspeed, Mach number, 'g' level, type of entry and loading. In addition to the stall warning discussed under Normal and Accelerated Stalls, a build up in side forces (a tendency to move the pilot to the side of the cockpit) will be encountered immediately prior to departure. These may not be detectable in a high speed, high 'g' condition where wing rock will be the most positive indication of impending departure. If AOA is not reduced to below stall, departures can be expected to develop into spins. The AOA at departure is highly dependent on loading. Clean or Sparrows-only aeroplanes will depart at slightly greater than 30 units, while heavy wing loaded air-to-ground configurations may depart as low as 27 to 28 units. Departures are best prevented by proper control of AOA. Although aileron deflection may aggravate the situation, excessive AOA is the primary cause of departure. Use of ailerons, or excessive rudder deflection at departure, increase the probability of spin entry following departure.

Departures are characterised by a yawing motion with roll in the direction of yaw. The yawing motion at departure will be more violent when encountered during a high speed, high 'g' condition. At the first indication of departure, or when a nose high, rapidly decaying airspeed situation is encountered, attempt to reduce AOA by moving the stick smoothly forward, simultaneously neutralising ailerons and rudder. The throttles should be retarded to idle to reduce the probability of engine flame out unless, in the pilot's opinion, the altitude is so low that thrust will be required to minimise altitude loss during the recovery. The stick should be smoothly, yet positively, moved forward; not jammed forward. Forward stick should be applied until negative 'g' is felt or until full forward stick is reached. The majority of recoveries will be effected before the stick reaches the forward stop. If recovery is not apparent after the application of full forward stick, deploy the drag chute without hesitation.

Large roll and yaw oscillations may be present during recoveries from departures. AOA indications will be erroneous during these oscillations and should not be used as a departure recovery indication. Applying full forward stick and neutralising ailerons and rudder is the most effective means of damping the oscillations and should be maintained until the oscillations cease. An out-of-control situation may be re-entered if stick movement off the forward stop is commenced prior to the aeroplane unloading and the oscillations ceasing. A series of rolls at 15 to 20 units AOA may be encountered with full forward stick; however, the unloading will not be present. Do not attempt to fly out of this condition, rather maintain full forward stick until negative 'g' is felt. Do not confuse the rolls with a spin. Maintain 5 to 10 units until airspeed is sufficient for dive pull out (approximately 200 knots). Use AOA to minimise altitude loss and do not exceed 19 units during pull out. (Note – Engine stall or flameouts may occur during departure; however, engine relights can be obtained with the throttles at idle even during a developed spin. Disengage the AFCS if in use.)

If AOA has been reduced to below the stall, the aeroplane will not spin. The drag chute should produce recovery shortly after deployment and will reduce the oscillations encountered during recovery. It is not necessary to jettison the chute since it will separate as airspeed builds up. The altitude loss following departure is dependent upon nose attitude at recovery, which is usually very nose low. Altitude loss following pulling out of a 90 degree dive, initiated at 200 knots and utilising 19 units, is approximately 5,000 ft.

SPINS

Spins have been entered from level flight stalls, accelerated turns, vertical climbs, 60 degree pullouts and inverted climbs. Departure and spin characteristics were investigated with a clean aeroplane, various heavy wing loadings and with asymmetric loads. The AOA indicator is the primary instrument for verifying the type of spin (upright or inverted). During upright spins, the AOA indicator will be pegged at 30 units and during inverted spins will indicate zero (0) units. The direction of spin can easily be determined from visual cues if ground reference is available; however, the direction of spin should be verified by referencing the turn needle (not the ball). The turn needle will always be pegged in the direction of the spin. (Note – AOA may momentarily indicate less than 30 units (off the peg) during a spin; however, a sustained yawing motion in one direction verifies the spin condition.) The Radar Intercept Officer (RIO) should relay airspeed and altitude information to the pilot continuously during uncontrolled flight. If the airspeed is increasing through 200 knots, the aeroplane is not spinning. Fly the aeroplane.

UPRIGHT SPINS

Steep Oscillatory Mode

The upright spin is oscillatory in pitch, roll and yaw. The aeroplane pitch attitude may vary from slightly above the horizon to 90 degrees nose down, and large roll angle excursions will be encountered. Yaw rate in the spin may vary between 10 and 80 degrees per second, while airspeed will vary between 80 and 150 knots. The altitude lost during an upright spin is approximately 2,000 ft per turn, and the spin turn rates average about 5 to 6 seconds per turn. Initially, spin oscillations may produce slightly uncomfortable accelerations in the cockpit; however, the oscillations should not be confusing. If recovery from the departure has not been effected after deploying the drag chute, and the aeroplane has been determined to be in an upright spin, POSITIVELY determine the spin direction and apply full aileron in the direction of the spin. Recovery from most spins will occur within two turns for a symmetrically loaded aeroplane. The upright spin recovery procedure is:

a) Positively determine spin direction.
b) Maintain full forward stick and neutral rudder, and apply full aileron in the direction of the spin (Right turn needle deflection, right spin, right aileron).
c) When the aeroplane unloads (negative 'g') and/or yaw rate stops, neutralise the ailerons and fly out of the unusual attitude.
d) Do not exceed 19 units during dive pull out.
e) If still out of control by 10,000 ft above terrain – EJECT.

The most positive indications of recovery from a spin is the aeroplane unloading. Incidents have been encountered, however, where the yaw rate stopped and the aeroplane entered 15 to 20 unit AOA rolls. If this occurs, the ailerons should be neutralised when the yaw rate stops and full forward stick maintained until the rolls cease and the aeroplane unloads. Large excursions in roll and yaw may be encountered during recovery; do not mistake these excursions for a spin direction reversal. If the aeroplane's nose remains on one spot on the ground or horizon, the aeroplane is rolling, not spinning. Spin direction reversals are rare using the recommended recovery procedure; however, if reversal occurs, again positively determine the spin direction and reapply the upright spin recovery procedure.

An out-of-control situation will be re-entered if aft stick pressure is applied prior to the aeroplane unloading and the oscillations ceasing. Maintain 5 to 10 units until airspeed is sufficient for dive pullout (approximately 200 knots). Total altitude loss from a departure that develops into a spin until level flight is achieved can be as little as 10,000 ft; however, it will be closer to 15,000 ft if too much time is consumed determining spin direction. If the pilot considers that there is insufficient altitude for recovery, the crew should eject immediately.

Flat Mode

There have been isolated cases of the aeroplane exhibiting an upright flat spin mode. The flat spin can develop within one or two turns after departure from controlled flight, or after several turns of an upright steep oscillatory spin. Oscillations in pitch and roll are not apparent in the flat spin. The spin turn rate is 3 to 4 seconds per turn, and the altitude lost per turn is 1,000 to 1,500 ft. There is no known technique for recovery from a flat spin. Tests indicate that a very high AOA, well in excess of 30 units, is required for flat spin entry. Proper use of controls at departure will preclude entering a flat spin.

INVERTED SPINS

The aeroplane is highly resistant to an inverted spin entry and tests indicate that pro-spin controls are necessary to maintain an inverted spin. The inverted spin is characterised by zero (0) units indicated AOA and negative 'g' and is less oscillatory than the upright steep oscillatory spin. Spin direction can be determined visually by the yawing motion of the aeroplane or more positively by the deflection of the turn needle which is always pegged in the direction of the spin. Airspeed will vary up to 150 knots. During an inverted spin, roll rate is opposite yaw rate and can cause pilots to misinterpret spin direction. If recovery from uncontrolled flight is not effected by utilising the out-of-control recovery procedure, and the aeroplane has been determined to be in an inverted spin, apply the following:

a) Positively determine the spin direction.
b) Full rudder against the spin (opposite the turn needle deflection).
c) Stabilator and ailerons neutral.
d) When the yaw rate stops, neutralise all controls and fly out of the unusual attitude.
e) Do not exceed 19 units AOA during recovery.
f) If still out-of-control at 10,000 ft AGL – EJECT.

The RIO should relay airspeed and altitude information to the pilot continuously during uncontrolled flight. This is particularly important in an apparent inverted spin, since airspeed may be the only recognisable difference between such a spin and a high speed inverted spiral. Rudder deflection at negative AOA causes roll opposite to rudder. After recovery from an inverted spin, continued rudder deflection will probably cause entry into an opposite inverted spiral. AOA and turn needle may cause the pilot to believe he is still in the spin as his interpretation of visual cues may be unreliable. The best indication that the aeroplane is in a spiral will be increasing airspeed and, possibly, high negative 'g' forces (depending on stabilator trim and position). If airspeed is increasing through 200 knots, the aeroplane is not spinning.

Chapter Ten

Accidents and Incidents

Like any other complex military aircraft the Phantom had its own particular quirks which could catch the unwary and lead to potentially dangerous situations. This chapter looks at some of the incidents that RAF Phantom crews had to cope with in the 1970s.

Uncommanded Control Movements (UCMs)

During the time the Phantom was in service with the RAF there were a number of incidents of uncommanded control movements whereby an aircraft's attitude was suddenly altered without any input from the pilot. Although these instances could be extremely disconcerting, they tended to vary in magnitude from minor inconveniences to situations which put the lives of the crew at risk. On one occasion a twin-stick Phantom was flying straight and level at 500 ft when the control column suddenly moved forward, pitching the aircraft towards the ground. The pilot was able to regain control immediately and, having ascertained that the control movement had not been initiated by the navigator, he initiated a climb to a safe height before switching off the stability augmentation in pitch and recovering to base. An investigation by the engineering section discovered that a pipe in the stabilator feel system had been forced during maintenance to produce a distortion that had weakened the sealant at a joint, as a result of which there had been a substantial leak in the feel system.

A more serious UCM occurred when a Phantom began to fishtail violently shortly after a night take-off. A PAN call was transmitted and the aircraft climbed to 4,500 ft. With the stability augmentation disengaged, the aircraft continued to yaw from side to side and also began to oscillate in pitch by up to 10 degrees. The necessary emergency drills were carried out, the centreline overload tank was jettisoned over the sea and the navigator began to switch off all non-essential electrics. The wing tanks were also jettisoned to reduce weight and allow a lower touchdown speed and the aircraft was set up for a straight-in approach for an emergency landing. During the approach the aircraft continued to yaw and pitch violently but the pilot was able to guide it onto the runway to make successful contact with the arrester gear. Following a report of fuel venting from the port wing, the engines were shut down on the runway. Once again an exhaustive engineering appraisal was carried out and although a number of minor defects were noted it was not possible to identify the actual cause of the UCM. On subsequent sorties the aircraft behaved impeccably and there was to be no repeat performance.

On another occasion a crew had just taken off as part of a pair when, with the undercarriage and flaps coming up, the pilot noticed that the control column was moving fore-and-aft all by itself. Although the stick movement was rapid, it was, at first, relatively mild but the oscillations soon increased in violence to the point where the control column was wrenched forward out of the pilot's hand. The aircraft pitched sharply nose down and rolled rapidly to the right before the pilot could disengage the stability augmentation system. This cured the immediate control problems although the aircraft still felt over-sensitive, particularly in roll. Having dumped fuel, the pilot carried out a low speed handling check before making a successful landing. The subsequent investigation found a number of faults with the aircraft's Automatic Flying Control System.

A UCM may have been the cause of a mid-air collision between two Phantoms of 228 OCU on 14 April 1982. A student pilot and a staff navigator in XT903 took off from Coningsby as the lead aircraft of a pair, the other aircraft being XT912, crewed by an OCU pilot with a student in the back seat. The brief had been for the pilot in XT912 to assume the lead after take-off and with the two aircraft in a gentle turn to the right at 1,000 ft he began to manoeuvre down and to the left to take up his position. Advancing the throttles slightly to prevent his aircraft falling too far behind, he suddenly became aware that the two aircraft were, in fact, getting dangerously close together. The convergence continued despite full forward stick and at the last moment the pilot applied full left aileron and left rudder in an attempt to prevent the canopy taking the brunt of the impact. Despite this, both canopies shattered and the aircraft rolled to the left and began to vibrate violently. The navigator ejected immediately after the collision but the pilot delayed his ejection by which time his aircraft was inverted and in a steep descent. It crashed near the village of Walcot, approximately five miles west of Coningsby.

The crew of XT903 had felt a thump but were not initially aware that this had been due to a collision, however a lack of communication with the other aircraft and a pall of black smoke on the ground soon made it clear what had happened. An inspection by another aircraft showed significant damage to the starboard wing trailing edge and tailplane, and that the right underwing tank was missing. The underside of the fuselage had also been damaged. The crew elected to jettison the left overload tank to avoid any asymmetric handling problems and due to the damage to the right wing, only made turns to the left. The recovery was relatively uneventful, the aircraft being brought to a halt by use of the runway arrester gear.

The collision could not be explained with any degree of certainty. The pilot of XT912 reported that his aircraft had pitched up without any input on his part and had then failed to respond when he moved the control column fully forward. From the wreckage that was recovered a technical malfunction could not be proved, but the accident report did acknowledge that there had been a number of cases of UCMs on the Phantom, some of which could not be explained.

TURBINE TROUBLES

As already related in Chapter Four, the Spey 202 suffered extreme reliability problems in the early 1970s caused mainly by defects in the engine's turbine. This led to numerous incidents, the level of danger depending on exactly when the failure occurred. On 12 October 1970 XT894 was taking off with a heavy external load, including full ammunition, when an explosion took place in the starboard engine. A loss of thrust was immediately apparent and Air Traffic Control (ATC) reported that the engine was on fire. At this point the aircraft had just become airborne at 170 knots and so the pilot was faced with an instant decision to abort the take-off or continue. He favoured the former course of action and immediately deployed the brake chute, applied full anti-skid braking and lowered the hook to take the Rotary Hydraulic Arrestor Gear (RHAG) which was engaged at around 130 knots. An examination of the starboard engine showed that there had been a failure of the low pressure turbine bearing, a known problem area. Had the hook not worked properly a potentially life threatening accident would undoubtedly have occurred. Problems had been experienced on the Phantom with the hook failing to lower on initial application, but on this occasion full movement had been checked prior to entering the active runway which may have been a factor in it working first time when it was really needed.

Another serious situation arose exactly a year later when Phantom FGR.2 XV479 of 54 Squadron was taking off from Karup in Denmark. Laden with full internal fuel and three external tanks, XV479 was the

No. 2 in a pair and at first the take off appeared normal. Reheat was disengaged at about 320 knots and the aircraft continued in full Military power. About four miles from the airfield, during a level turn onto the outbound heading at about 550 ft and 360 knots, the pilot felt a surge and noticed a very high over-temperature of the port engine. The engine was immediately throttled to idle and the temperature began to reduce.

With speed decaying towards 300 knots, the pilot tried to engage reheat on the starboard engine, but without success. By now the aircraft was down to 300 ft and 260 knots and with the situation becoming critical the navigator was told to eject. The pilot made one last attempt to get full reheat, but again the engine failed to light up. Accordingly, he too ejected and after a total flight time of three minutes the Phantom crashed in a level attitude and bounced into a farmhouse, killing two occupants. The crew ejections were successful, although the navigator was injured. During the short flight no engine overheat or fire light captions had illuminated. Both engines were to Blue Standard and de-rated to STI Spey 31 and investigations showed that the port engine had suffered a burn out of the HP2 turbine, possibly as a result of over-fuelling. No definite reason could be found as to why the starboard reheat failed to light, although malfunction of the fuel system was suspected.

If an engine was going to fail, the best time for it to happen was at the end of a sortie when the aircraft's weight would have been considerably lower and it was likely that plenty of height would still be available, allowing time to take the appropriate action. This happened to the crew of XV571 on 22 September 1972 when a rumbling noise was heard coming from the starboard engine as they were returning to their home airfield. With JPT rising and the engine low pressure warning light illuminated, the pilot shut down the troublesome engine. Shortly after shutdown the internal fire warning light came on but went out again after about two minutes. No further difficulty was encountered and the pilot completed a successful single-engine landing. It was discovered that there had been a failure of the starboard engine HP1 turbine bearing which had also resulted in local burning of the aircraft's external skin behind the engine cooling air outlet duct leading to Cat 3 damage.

FUMES IN THE COCKPIT

There were several instances of fumes seeping into the cockpit during flight and in the worst case these very nearly led to crew incapacitation. A Phantom was engaged on an air combat sortie at 20,000 ft when the front and then the rear cockpits filled with clear, acidic fumes. The fumes were extremely irritating and the pilot was forced to take his hands off the control column and throttle to protect his eyes. Even so his vision was impaired to the extent that he was unable to read the instruments and the horizon was only visible because the weather conditions were clear, thus allowing a sharp distinguishing line between sky and sea. Both crew members felt a burning sensation on the uncovered skin around their faces and wrists. Such was the level of discomfort that another Phantom had to act as a shepherd aircraft and assisted the pilot to make a successful landing. The source of the fumes was not established although the cabin conditioning turbine, which had often been the cause of noxious gases in the past, was removed for further testing. The problem did not recur during a subsequent air test, or during the sorties that followed.

The crew of another Phantom were at 4,000 ft when the navigator noticed an unusual smell in the cockpit. Both crew immediately selected 100 per cent oxygen but shortly afterwards the pilot became dizzy and disorientated. He put out a PAN call and made to return to base, but very soon his condition began to deteriorate. Suspecting oxygen contamination he removed his mask, however, this had no effect and he reported that everything appeared to be happening in slow motion. His navigator was also in trouble and both found it difficult to make decisions. While going through the pre-landing checks the aircraft suddenly lost height and at 200 ft on finals the pilot sensed that he was inverted and overshot. This manoeuvre proved to be extremely difficult to perform as the pilot was convinced that he was moving the control column the wrong way. His second approach was low and fast but the aircraft successfully engaged the arrester gear at the approach end of the runway.

The capacity of the crew to carry out decisions had been severely impaired to the extent that they had great difficulty in performing the after landing checks and on vacating the aircraft were unable to stand without assistance. Subsequently they developed severe headaches which persisted for over three hours. In this case the cabin conditioning system was not found to be defective and there was no indication of oxygen contamination. Although the source of the fumes could not be fully established, it was felt that the most likely cause was a defective component of the radar which had overheated.

HYDRAULIC FAILURES

The very first Phantom FGR.2 to be lost in RAF service was XV395 which crashed on 9 July 1969. After a simulated HiLoHi strike sortie, the crew were returning to Coningsby and had just intercepted the glidepath under precision approach radar (PAR) control when several unusual instrument readings were observed. The pneumatics gauge was seen to be registering 5,000 psi instead of 3,000 psi, and both Power Control hydraulic pressure readings had dropped to 2,000 psi from the normal 3,000 psi. The pilot warned the navigator that he might have to eject and increased power to 85 per cent prior to transmitting a Mayday call. The utility hydraulics pressure remained steady at 3,000 psi but both PC-1 and PC-2 pressures continued to fall and at 1,000 psi the controls began to stiffen. At this point the navigator was given the command to eject which he did at about 1,700 ft and 190 knots.

By the time that the aircraft was approaching 1,400 ft control stiffening had progressed to the extent that with 500 psi on PC-1 and less on PC-2 the pilot could not lift the starboard wing which was now 15 degrees low. As the situation was becoming irrecoverable, he too ejected. Both the pilot and navigator made safe landings without serious injury. It was subsequently concluded that the false readings of the PC-1 and 2 and pneumatic gauges had been the result of failure of an electrical connection, and that the control stiffening was the outcome of a jamming valve in the return line common to the PC-1 and PC-2 system. As a result of this accident valves of an improved design by the Kohler company were fitted to RAF Phantoms.

Ever since the adoption of the retractable undercarriage, any malfunction of the landing gear had been high on the list of safety issues, especially with the ever increasing performance of military aircraft. On one occasion the pilot of a Phantom FG.1 had returned to base after a night air defence sortie and had just raised the gear following a roller landing when his aircraft suffered a hydraulic failure. On the downwind leg of the circuit both main undercarriage legs locked down but there was no corresponding green light from the nosewheel indicator. Fuel was only sufficient for a further three circuits before the minimum required for landing was reached. As a result of the failure the pilot had been deprived of a number of services including the normal operation of flaps, undercarriage, wheelbrakes, rudder power, anti-skid and nosewheel steering, however, emergency air was available to extend the undercarriage and to provide emergency wheel braking. During a flypast of the control tower the nosewheel was seen to be trailing at an angle of about 45 degrees to the fuselage.

This posed something of a dilemma. With directional control likely to be difficult after touchdown an arrested landing was recommended, however, the normal drill for landing with an unsafe nose leg was that an arrest should not be made. The Duty Officer Flying advised the crew that a cable engagement would be extremely hazardous because of the risk of the cable either riding up over the nose or snagging on some part of the airframe if the nose leg collapsed before the aircraft passed the cable.

Despite this potential hazard the pilot elected to go for an arrested landing and positioned his aircraft on long finals for a shallow flapless approach with a datum speed of 180 KCAS. Because of the difficulty of flying such an unusual approach at night, the aircraft touched down 700 feet short of the cable which was engaged by the hook at an estimated 160 knots with the nose slightly above the horizontal. After the wire was engaged the nose pitched down sharply and contacted the runway about 400 feet beyond the cable. The crew did not suffer any injuries and the aircraft was subsequently assessed as having Cat 3 damage. It was later found that the accident had been caused by a longitudinal crack in part of the nose leg assembly which had allowed a progressive loss of fluid and ultimately system failure.

Hydraulic failures were a recurring problem with the Phantom as Group Captain Mike Shaw recalls.

> The Utility Hydraulic System, for the services and ancillaries, was complex and prone to failure more often than the two Power Controls Systems, though all operated at 3,000 psi. During my time with the US Marine Corps one of our F-4Bs suffered repeated Utility failures, leading to the need to make emergency hookwire engagements. The failures all occurred about thirty minutes into the flights, but no trace of hydraulic fluid leak was found.
>
> Eventually an SNCO [Senior Non-Commissioned Officer] tracked down the fault to a cracked end-cap on a transfer pump in a fuselage fuel tank (there were six of them), which was allowing fluid to leak into the fuel. The exhaust smoke trail from the J79s may have been blacker than usual, and some pilots had had practice at emergency arrested landings, but no harm was done. However, ten years later the same mystery afflicted one of the RAF's Phantom FGR.2s on 228 OCU at Coningsby. My diagnosis of the fault amazed the Senior Engineering Officer and gave me a reprehensibly smug feeling. You can never tell when even the most obscure experience can come in useful!

Electrical Problems

It is often said that crews really begin to earn their money when things start to go wrong. After being airborne for about an hour on 13 October 1971, the crew of XV577 were presented with a bewildering array of equipment failures. At the time the Stability Augmentation System was engaged but the Auto Pilot had been switched off, and at the onset of trouble the pilot reported that the aircraft pitched slightly. Almost immediately a whole series of warning captions illuminated – Primary Gyro Off, IFF (Identification Friend or Foe) Fail, both Inlet Guide Vane Malfunction and Windscreen Overheat. In addition, the pilot's attitude indicators and horizontal situation indicator (HSI) were frozen, maximum engine rpm was limited to 88 per cent, the left fuel flow indicated 70 lb/min with the right fuel flow at 20 lb/min, the PC-1 hydraulic reading had fallen to 300 psi and there was no response to a selection of half flap using the normal system. Meanwhile in the rear cockpit the navigator was faced with eight circuit breakers which were repeatedly tripping out.

In the early stages of the incident the crew suspected Bleed Duct failure as the symptoms tallied with those described in the Flight Reference Cards. The aircraft returned to base in formation with another aircraft and made a successful approach and RHAG engagement. An initial investigation revealed air in the PC-1 hydraulic system which accounted for the low reading of that one gauge, but the bleed air system was proved to be fully serviceable. Before this particular sortie the aircraft had been worked on for a recurring right generator malfunction and although no generator warnings had occurred during the flight, the investigation was then concentrated on the electrical generating system.

After ten days of exhaustive trouble shooting nothing conclusive had been found, although the left Voltage Regulator/Supervisory Panel (VRSP) was suspected. The VRSP could not be faulted when tested on the ground but it was decided to fly the suspected components in an aircraft known to be serviceable. Before flight the Ram Air Turbine (RAT) was proven, and as an added precaution the suspect VRSP was fitted to the right side of the test aircraft as less important systems were powered from this side. During the test flight the VRSP did indeed prove to be defective, but only above 31,000 ft.

INSTRUMENT FAILURE

When flying in cloud the pilot is dependent on the instruments giving him the correct information as it would not take long for his own senses to 'topple' and for him to lose control. On 1 June 1973 XV397 of 17 Squadron was returning from a singleton sortie and descending in cloud to level at 2,000 ft, the pilot having carried out the necessary vital actions prior to lowering the undercarriage and full flap. With the aircraft at 200 knots he noticed an ADI OFF caption with the associated master caution light. He attempted to stabilise at 180 knots and 2,000 ft using the secondary attitude indicator (SAI), but almost immediately the altimeter indicated a descent despite the fact that the SAI was still showing the aircraft to be straight and level.

Although he increased power and tried to ease the nose up, the pilot could not prevent the descent increasing and at about 1,000 ft he ordered the navigator to eject, before ejecting himself. Tragically, the navigator was killed when his ascending seat collided with the underside of the pilot's jettisoned canopy. The subsequent inquiry concluded that the accident had been caused by failure of both the main and standby attitude indicators which at the time had a common power source and could, by selection, have a common reference system. Action was already in hand to provide an SAI with its own reference system and this accident only served to add further emphasis to the requirement.

BIRDSTRIKES

As the Phantom was initially used in the low level role by the RAF, birdstrikes were a particular hazard. Air intakes, wing leading edges, underwing stores and canopies were especially at risk and many incidents that occurred when flying at high speed resulted in Cat 3 damage. Should the unfortunate bird be ingested into an engine, then a replacement engine would have to be fitted, a situation that was guaranteed to cause even more headaches for the Engineering staff in the early 1970s as there was already a serious shortage of Spey engines (see Chapter Four).

A potentially serious situation occurred on 24 May 1972 and involved XV486 which was in the lead of a 'battle four' at 500 ft AGL and 420 knots. Moments after lifting his visor to identify another aircraft, the pilot was hit in the face by the remains of a bird which had shattered the right side of the front windscreen. The bird was seen immediately before it hit, but the pilot only had time to lower his head and close his eyes before he was struck by the debris. Having pulled up and reduced speed, the pilot turned towards base but was unable to see out of his right eye and could not communicate with his navigator, nor hear any instructions because of the noise caused by the hole in the windscreen. Engine and instrument readings were normal and during recovery the pilot regained vision in his right eye and was able to land without further incident. Given the circumstances the pilot was lucky to escape with a slight injury and this incident emphasised the need for a double visor system so that a clear or tinted visor could be selected to suit conditions.

RICOCHETS

A further danger during low level operations was that caused by ricochets during practice shoots at ground targets. Crews had to be well practiced in the art of air-to-ground firing and although range procedures were strict, there was still the possibility of ricochets causing airframe damage during the pullout manoeuvre. On 3 December 1970 a very experienced Canadian Air Force pilot on an exchange tour with 6 Squadron was leading a pair of Phantoms on a weapons training mission on the Cowden range. In a 15 degree dive the pilot opened and ceased firing at 3,000 ft and 2,500 ft respectively and made a normal 4g recovery. It was during this recovery manoeuvre that a thump on the airframe was felt and heard. The leader's aircraft (XV466) was inspected by his No. 2 who could see no sign of any impact, but on landing it was discovered that the aircraft had sustained Cat 3 damage to the area around the port air intake.

A similar incident occurred to XT909 on 6 October 1972 during rocket firing at 650 ft AGL from a 10 degree dive profile. A 4 g pull out was sufficient to bring the aircraft out of its dive above the 500 ft safety height, but when climbing away from the target at about 850 ft a ricochet hit was felt. Another aircraft reported damage to the right intake ramp and this was soon followed by occasional coughing, banging and rpm dipping from the starboard engine, accompanied by spasmodic yawing. The engine was shut down and the aircraft landed without further incident. As XV468 had also been hit by a ricochet during air-to-ground gunnery six months before, it was recommended that the recovery manoeuvre be increased to 5 g as insurance against further incidents.

INADVERTENT SPIN

Although all fast-jet pilots should always expect the unexpected, a 228 OCU student on his first conversion flight in a Phantom on 15 October 1971 was probably not thinking that he would be faced with a spin, even less an ejection situation. During a general handling sortie the student had completed an acceleration in reheat to 0.95 M and was in the process of decelerating when the Instructor took control and made a rapid entry to a steep left turn. The aircraft was held in buffet through about 90 degrees when it suddenly flicked to the left. Despite the Instructor initiating immediate recovery action, the incipient spin developed to a full upright spin to the left which subsequently became flat. As there was no known recovery action for a flat spin the crew ejected at around 12,000 ft, the aircraft (XT904) continuing to spin until it hit the sea near Cromer. Both student and Instructor were picked up by an SAR helicopter. The Board of Inquiry was of the view that the initial flick roll was caused by a stability augmentation transient but, despite being surprised and disorientated, the Instructor should have been able to prevent the aircraft departing into a fully developed spin (see Chapter Nine for a full description of the Phantom's spin characteristics).

LOW LEVEL FRIGHTS

Even after the RAF switched the Phantom from ground attack and strike operations to air defence it was often operated at low to medium levels as, by now, the threat of the high flying bomber had been replaced by aircraft capable of penetrating UK airspace flying fast and low in an attempt to delay detection and achieve surprise. For the crews there was the thrill of operating much closer to the ground, but there were inherent risks from flying at relatively low levels as are apparent in the following incidents.

On 12 March 1971 a four-ship formation of Phantoms, including XV412, was tasked to drop 1,000 lb bombs in level flight on the range at Vliehors, involving transit out and back over the North Sea. Weather conditions were poor with a visibility of around 5,000 metres in haze with a shallow layer of sea fog on the surface. Above lay a solid overcast at around 3,000 ft. The Phantoms flew out in battle formation, all pilots having to concentrate hard to maintain their position because of the haze. Eventually Vliehors appeared through the murk and all aircraft dropped their stores. On the way back the visibility appeared to improve slightly allowing the formation to spread out to around 2,000 yards between each aircraft, at which point the leader commenced a turn to the left. The pilot of the No. 3 Phantom had a quick look at his radio altimeter, saw a height of 2,000 ft, and then followed his leader through a turn of around 30 degrees. Having checked the new course with his navigator, he looked once more at the lead Phantom which again appeared to be in a left turn as he could see its underside. Instinctively he rolled on left bank once more before having a quick look at the instruments which showed that he was in a descending left turn at 450 knots with the altimeter rapidly passing through 500 ft. Levelling the wings, he pulled back hard on the control column and watched the rad alt continue to unwind, the aircraft eventually bottoming out at 300 ft above sea level. Having regained control, a very shaken pilot was able to resume his position in the formation and the rest of the flight was uneventful.

On reflection it soon became apparent that the lack of a visible horizon had played a large part in the incident and as the No. 3 had been forced to use his leader's aircraft as an attitude reference, he had inadvertently allowed his aircraft to descend. When the leader rolled out of his turn the No. 3 was thus below his leader and the sight of the underside of the lead aircraft created the illusion that he was turning once more when, in fact, he was flying straight and level. As the navigator had been fully occupied monitoring his radar displays he was not aware of the sudden height loss which amounted to approximately 1,800 ft in just a few seconds. But for a cry of "PULL OUT" from the No. 4 in the formation there could well have been another unexplained accident to add to the statistics.

Incidents could also occur during the best of weather. On a perfect summers day with scattered fair weather cumulus, excellent visibility and light winds, four Phantom crews briefed for an overland 2 versus 2 practice interception. Two aircraft were to fly a Combat Air Patrol with the other two flying as targets along a defined route. Not long after becoming airborne the No. 2 of those designated as fighters had its radar go unserviceable, but the sortie was continued as the squadron's operating procedures covered such a situation by placing the onus on the leader to guide the No. 2 to a position in which it could use its AIM-9D Sidewinder heat-seeking missiles. As this type of attack had to be carried out from the rear, a hard 180 degree turn would have to be executed on visual contact with the target.

Not long after setting up the CAP, the fighter leader called that he had a low level contact and the two went into the attack. Sighting a target at 3 nm and slightly to the right, the pilot of the No. 2 called 'Tally Ho' and began his attack. As the lateral displacement was insufficient for a 180 degree turn in level flight he was forced to use the vertical and pulled up into a wing-over to the right using full cold power. On lowering the nose during the completion of the manoeuvre it quickly became apparent that the ground was rapidly getting closer and there was a distinct danger that the Phantom would fly straight in. The pilot's initial reaction was to pull back hard on the control column but this quickly increased the angle of attack to the point where the aircraft began to lose speed and enter buffet. The rate of descent was the same as before. It took a conscious effort on the part of the pilot to reduce the amount of back stick to lower the angle of attack to the optimum value. At the same time he selected full reheat. The aircraft began to respond and it eventually pulled out with around 150 feet to spare.

One factor that emerged in the post-flight debrief was that the pilot had been used to flying clean wing Phantoms whereas the low level sortie was flown with three overload tanks which increased the amount of fuel carried by around 40 per cent. This considerably increased the aircraft's weight and adversely affected its handing characteristics, particularly at high angles of attack. The situation was made worse by rising ground. As the target had been running along a valley the wing-over had taken the F-4 over the valley side so that the descent was into an area approximately 1,000 ft higher than the valley floor. The combination of unexpectedly sluggish turning performance and rising ground had produced a very close call.

Great care also had to be taken when flying the Phantom at high angles of attack as Group Captain Mike Shaw recalls.

> All F-4s have similar lateral flying controls: stick left, port spoilers rise, starboard aileron goes down and vice versa. It works well, subsonic and supersonic, except at high AOA. The spoilers travel from flush to 45 degrees up, the aileron from 1 degree up to 30 degrees down. If a wing is at high AOA, near the stall, the harsh use of aileron may stall it, and instead of lifting the wing, it will cause it to drop. Meanwhile the spoilers on the other wing will be up, spoiling the lift on that side too! If the stick is held over, the aircraft can lose enough lift to fly, or else might roll hard either way. At high AOA and/or in deep buffet, the stick had to be kept laterally neutral with rudder alone being used for roll control. It was quite a trap.

EJECT, EJECT!

One thing that is drummed into fighter crews from a very early stage in their training is that in the event of an irrecoverable emergency, it is imperative to get out quickly as a delay of even a second or two might be the difference between life and death. Flight Lieutenants Pat Watling and Steve 'Sid' James of 111 Squadron were faced with just such a situation on 3 June 1980 but, happily, the only statistics they added to were those compiled by Martin Baker, manufacturer of the world's foremost ejection seats.

The two had been engaged in dissimilar air combat training with an F-5 of the 525th Aggressor Squadron based at RAF Alconbury and were flying XV589 'P', an ex Royal Navy FG.1. The sortie passed off uneventfully and Watling returned to Alconbury where he carried out a run and break before settling the Phantom onto a visual approach. When on finals to land, however, the nose of the Phantom was seen to be moving and the radome swung round to the right on its hinge until it was pointing backwards towards the starboard engine intake. The disruption of the airflow meant that the aircraft began a slow roll to the right which had to be counteracted by the use of port rudder, as any significant aileron input at the relatively high angle of attack prior to landing would most likely have produced adverse yaw and a roll in the opposite direction. With the aircraft at around 200 ft and still descending, Watling only had a few seconds to decide what to do. He quickly came to the conclusion that the only alternative was to eject, but there was not enough time to inform his navigator. In such a situation the back-seater was trained to leave the aircraft immediately after he saw the pilot eject and in this particular case both vacated the aircraft successfully, coming down not far from the main East Coast railway line which runs along the eastern boundary of the airfield.

The subsequent investigation found that the accident had been caused by failure of the radome locking mechanism which had allowed it to open in flight. As a former Fleet Air Arm aircraft the nose would have been regularly opened to allow it to be taken from the flight deck to the hangar on HMS *Ark Royal* and over a period of time the locking catch had become weakened to the point where it ultimately failed. A priority check on the other ex Navy Phantoms at Leuchars found a number with similarly defective catches.

Chapter Eleven

Crew Debrief – 1

In the early days of Phantom operations in RAF Germany the F-4 took over the role of nuclear strike from the Canberra B.I.8, in addition to ground attack using conventional weapons. Having become closely acquainted with the Phantom at Boscombe Down, Peter Desmond, by now a Squadron Leader, found himself at Bruggen in the role of O.C. Navigation and Planning (Nav and Plans) with a lot of work to do to build the station up to operational status.

Although it had no aircraft and the runway still belonged to the contractors, Bruggen in the Spring of 1970 was the most exciting base in the RAF. Due west of Dusseldorf, just on the German side of the Dutch border, it had been closed for nine months awaiting the arrival of the Phantoms with their duel role capability of Strike (nuclear) and Attack (conventional) weapons delivery. They also had a tertiary role as air defence fighters but were unlikely to be used in that role other than for local air base defence. Previously the Canberras based in Germany had been Strike only and were tasked to react either individually (selective release) as a demonstration of intent, or, finally, in one huge wave when it would be all over bar the mushroom clouds. Under the new NATO doctrine of 'appropriate response', a graduated reply to Warsaw Pact aggression was the thing. Starting on the dual role with new aircraft from empty sheds was an immense task. We were given a year to get ready for a dual role evaluation by a multi-national team and, if successful, the Wing would be assigned Combat Ready status. Failure was out of the question.

The Station Commander was specially selected (a navigator) Group Captain John Curtiss (later Air Marshal Sir John KBE, KCB) and he was the man for the occasion. The first to form was 14 Squadron, commanded by Wing Commander John Sutton (later Air Marshal Sir John and Lieutenant Governor of Jersey) in June 1970 followed by 17 Squadron under Wing Commander Paddy Hine (later Air Chief Marshal Sir Patrick) two months later. The Wing was completed by the formation of 31 Squadron commanded by Wing Commander Chris Sprent the following year.

Nav and Plans was based around the centralised mission planning centre, yet to be built, equipped, staffed and trained, and would include the existing Intelligence Flight and the first ever RAF Radar Prediction Centre. Together with my boss, Wing Commander Denis Allison, whom I had known on 87 Squadron Meteors at Wahn, I travelled all over Germany and the Benelux air bases seeing how they went about the task and we began to get some idea. Flight Lieutenant Norman Hughes was posted in as the Radar Prediction Officer and we had to send him to the West German Air Force and then to the Munich manufacturers of the terrain models used in the prediction process. A set of offices and storerooms had to be found for his department, and the rig for the travelling camera, which took the shadow pictures for the predicted flight path, had to be made by our own engineers.

Radar prediction was needed in addition to the inertial system because, in order to release a nuclear weapon in non-visual conditions, two independent means of verifying position were necessary. All this had to come together to enable us to produce two combat mission folders, containing everything needed to fly the mission, and brief the aircrew, in under 60 minutes. During this planning period the crew were being briefed on the latest intelligence and the nuclear weapon was being broken out of the special storage area, to be transferred by armed guard convoy to the loading bay. The weapon remained under US control until the NATO and National release codewords were given and independently verified by both nations. Only then was the weapon released to the crew. The speed with which the mission had to be planned necessitated a network of pre-planned legs which took us to the nearest point to the target, from which we could do the minimum new planning necessary. As soon as they knew the target, and the type of burst required, the crew had to choose the delivery profile and we could do little until they decided. Of course everyone was hovering over them as they deliberated and then had to leap into frantic action once the decision had been made. It was a gigantic task, but we did it.

I was able to organise a series of flights in an Army Air Corps Beaver along our side of the Inner German Border (the official name for the Iron Curtain) to examine our pre-planned targets along the zone border. This was to such good effect that we had several border violations filed against us on one sortie. In fact we did not deliberately infringe their side of the Inner German Boundary, but we came very close. I recall flying at 200 feet along a country road where the ditch on the eastern side formed the boundary. I then organised it for the squadron crews which went down well. Subsequently I had the idea of flying the crews (and me) to Berlin and back so that they could see their pre-planned Soviet airfield targets, a trip which included a low level flight all around Berlin itself, still under multinational military control.

No. 31 Squadron was commanded by Wing Commander Chris Sprent who recalls some of the difficulties that had to be overcome during the early period of Phantom operations.

At the time, the Phantom, in RAF guise, was experiencing major problems with its Spey engines, and to a lesser extent its nav/attack system. Ferranti provided the INAS and, compared to modern electronics, it was pretty unreliable. The need to operate from carriers (and perhaps to supply work for Rolls-Royce) required the use of two reheated Speys to provide sufficient thrust, but how we suffered the consequences. The shortage of engines meant that either the formation of the squadron would have to be delayed or the OCU closed down for a while. Fortunately the second option prevailed. While it meant that we never achieved our full complement of crews in my three years on 31 Squadron, we benefited from the arrival of two experienced OCU instructors.

The first squadron members to arrive at Bruggen were Graham Gibb and David Pollington from No. 8 Course. They had a difficult time because Nos. 14 and 17 Squadrons, which had been established some months earlier, were working up for the station's first Taceval [Tactical Evaluation] with the Phantom. Our needs had a lower priority and hard graft was needed to obtain basic facilities. Following the arrival of aircraft, and air and ground crews, our first priority was to learn and to be declared in the strike (nuclear) role, so that we could mount QRA [Quick Reaction Alert]. This was the period when NATO was implementing a policy of flexible response to Warsaw Pact aggression, whereas previously deterrence had relied solely on a nuclear trip-wire. The new strategy required that we disperse aircraft, provide ground defences, build in redundancy in all aspects of support (culminating in the cleft stick!) and be proficient in the wide range of conventional weapons carried by the Phantom.

This called for initiative and original thought (if not larceny). Two challenges we could not do much about were the system of servicing at Bruggen and married accommodation. At that time semi-centralised servicing meant that an aircraft with a snag that could not be fixed at first line was towed the mile or so to the Engineering Wing from whence it could be recovered the next morning, if we were lucky. To launch a four-ship on the first wave was a rarity and matters did not usually improve as the day progressed. By the time we formed, married accommodation at Bruggen was fully occupied so many of our people had to live off base, often at some distance. This made it difficult to react to call-outs as quickly as the other squadrons.

Our nuclear weapons were American so there were two fingers on the trigger. During my time on 31 Squadron we developed two procedures using 1,000 lb bombs over and above normal dive and laydown deliveries. One was to toss slick (unretarded) 1,000 lb bombs against airfield targets to avoid dangerous over-flying of defences. The other was to drop a retarded weapon in the path of a fighter approaching low level from behind. During the time I was C.O. Hugh Kennedy and our nav leader David Hodges were killed during a night Taceval on the range at Vliehors. We keenly felt their loss.

With the Phantom we spent millions of pounds providing an aircraft with a ground attack/Strike capability which then had a relatively short life in this role. Number 31 Squadron only had the Phantom for five years before re-equipping with the Jaguar. The aircraft was quite difficult to fly compared to, say, the Lightning. One reason was that, for carrier operations, it had 'blown' flaps to reduce landing speed, which complicated throttle control on the approach.

As in all activities (and especially military ones), there were good times as well as the not so good. Our reward was to fly an exciting aircraft in three demanding roles – as often as possible! I expect life on 31 Squadron is little different today.

After his tour at Bruggen, Peter Desmond returned to the UK in early 1974 prior to becoming a Flight Commander with 43 Squadron at Leuchars. Before taking up his post there were a number of courses to attend, including the OCU course at Coningsby.

I was made welcome on 43 Squadron, then under the command of Wing Commander Jerry Cohu. After disembarkation leave, I had to take the Aviation Medicine Course at North Luffenham which was followed by the Sea Survival Course at Mountbatten, which was interesting if a touch chilly when we came to the immersion bit in the English Channel. The big course was the official Phantom OCU at Coningsby, which was scheduled to last for three months and started with two weeks of ground school. Coningsby summed up all that was depressing about winter in the Lincolnshire fens. Mist, rain and fog or, to put it another way, fog, rain and mist. Many of the ex Bruggen aircrew had returned to staff positions at the OCU and their characters seemed to change overnight. Coningsby did that to people.

I could do air-to-air intercepts standing on my head, I had been doing them since 1953, I knew the aircraft well, and I found no difficulty in the air. The problem arose on the ground afterwards when I had to explain why I had done something which had worked out fine, and I couldn't explain it because I didn't know. I was in serious danger of failing the course when I met up with Squadron Leader John Allison (later Air Marshal Sir John) who had the sense to realise that I had no problem, I just did things naturally. Before he took over, the OCU was in danger of being highjacked by a number of theoretical gurus who thought that talking about the geometry of the intercept was more important than being able to do it. The funny thing was that all their theories depended on an ideal non-evading target travelling at Mach 0.8 which was rarely found in real life.

As a potential Flight Commander, I had no pilot of my own, so I crewed up for the duration of the course with Tom Stonor, an old friend of mine, a former Canberra pilot and slated to take command of 31 Squadron at Bruggen. Tom was highly intelligent and rather diffident, had an endless fund of stories and was great fun to be with. Before his first solo we flew five sorties in the simulator and, on every occasion, he crashed on take-off. He was seriously concerned about this and was convinced that he would have a major problem when the time came to do it in the real thing; in vain did people tell him that the simulator was not true to type at low speeds. In the event all went well and a very happy Tom was seen walking back to the crewroom from his first trip.

It was at Coningsby that I started a series of emergencies which led to the eventual rumour that I did all my intercepts in the simulator and my emergencies in the air. On my first trip with Tom, his first solo, we had a major hydraulic system failure which he coped with admirably after my recitation from the Flight Reference Cards (this was the navigator's job in an emergency). It is worth noting that the three Phantom hydraulic systems, which ran at 3,000 lb/sq.in, were routed through a system of alloy pipes which had many right angle bends making fatigue failures inevitable. Eventually all these pipes were replaced by stainless steel pipes in a major modification programme after several aircraft had been lost.

One thing that I had not done before in the Phantom was air-to-air visual combat, which took the aircraft through the complete performance envelope, up to 7 g and Mach 1.4 at that time. A great deal of rubbish was talked about it, accompanied by hard to follow diagrams on the blackboard, and I have to admit that on my first two trips I really did not know what was going on. I had been completely disorientated from the commencement of combat and I really had no idea what had happened. The sheer physical effort involved was greater than any other activity that I had known and to maintain some degree of spatial awareness required expert tuition and much practice. I went to see John Allison and we agreed that he would put me up with his best combat pilot, Major Jim Schnabel, USAF, a Vietnam combat veteran, against the two staff pilots that I had previously flown with, who had baffled me so completely. Jim was wonderful, he was totally in command of the situation at all times and was able to take the time to explain what he was doing and why. We fought solo against the other two who were supposed to act as a pair and we disposed of them one at a time, after which I was quite happy when combat was discussed.

With the OCU course completed successfully, Peter Desmond headed north to join 43 Squadron, the famous Fighting Cocks who were based at Leuchars.

43 Squadron seemed to move in a world of its own. It was (and is) generally held by all present and former Fighting Cocks, of whatever rank, that the other squadrons were just unfortunate and that some divine smile beamed down on 43. They were not far wrong either. As the senior Flight Commander, I was the deputy Squadron Commander to Wing Commander Keith Beck, very talented and born with a touch of greatness, if a little impulsive at times. We got on well from the start and it was obvious that we were in for a hell of a ride. The problem was that Leuchars, although great for flying, was still in the dark ages as far as ground defence and Taceval was concerned, and it was going to be the task of Al Winkles, the other Flight Commander, and myself to shake the branches a bit. For a start we had to leave our comfortable hangar and start to operate out of dispersal, with all that nasty barbed wire and slit trenches. We even buried a bus to act as a crewroom. This was unpopular, as was the

idea of standing guard over the aircraft in the northern winter, but it had to be done. UK operations were going to be different from now on, with the possibility of a long drawn out conventional struggle, and we were in the front line.

43 Squadron was assigned to the control of SACLANT [Supreme Allied Commander Atlantic] and specialised in maritime air defence as well as normal UK air defence. This meant long sorties over the North Sea and the Atlantic, protecting convoys and Task Groups, supported by Airborne Early Warning Shackletons and Victor tankers. Anything up to seven hours was the norm. Leuchars Wing had to keep two fully armed aircraft and crews at ten minutes readiness for Quick Reaction Alert (QRA) for 24 hours per day, 365 days per year, in case of any incursion by unauthorised aircraft into UK airspace. The UK region was constantly probed by Soviet Badger, or more probably, Bear aircraft, and launches were frequent and very exciting for everyone. Shortly after I arrived a purpose built QRA complex was finished and we were able to move the alert aircraft, crews and groundcrew into accommodation designed for the job. Everything gave way to the alert in progress when the hooter went and, although we normally had some warning of a launch to come, as the intruder passed through the Norwegian system, occasionally we had a cold launch from ten minutes readiness when an intruder popped up, often a pair of Bears returning from Cuba and entering our territory from the south west. The sight of your first Bear with the tremendous resonance from all those props was unforgettable. The Victor tanker used to follow up behind us to try and get a glimpse and we developed a special comradeship with those guys. We always had to keep sufficient fuel on board to get back to Leuchars which often meant having to start the return journey with 12,500 pounds of fuel remaining (BINGO fuel), because of the great distances from base.

The Phantom FG.1 with which we were equipped was far from ideal for the task of long over water sorties as it had no inertial navigation equipment and no HF radio. The radar had a mapping range of 200 miles and on one memorable occasion, in an aircraft returning from mid Atlantic, the pilot spotted a coastline at the limit of the 200 mile range scale and asked if that was Scotland only to be told that it was the south west tip of Ireland. We were certainly the long rangers all right. We did take sandwiches and the aptly named 'Piddlepak', but having a pee in the cockpit wearing a bunny suit, an immersion suit, parachute and seat harness was an evening's entertainment. The immersion suit had rubber bootees attached which gave a whole new meaning to the expression 'Fill yer Boots'. Keith Beck and I shared our first experience of a Bear intercept one brilliant night when, having completed the intercept, we returned to the tanker to top up and were then told to go home. We had 18,000 lb of fuel on board so we lit both afterburners, went supersonic, and hightailed it for Scotland, just like riding a rocket, lighting up the starlit sky. Checking the fuel some minutes later, I was aghast to find that we were down to 7,000 lb, so we cancelled the burners and crept carefully home. It would have been difficult to explain the Squadron C.O. and his deputy running out of fuel having just topped up from the tanker. A Phantom in full afterburner used 2,300 lb of fuel per minute and the gauges tended to overread by 1,000 lb with the burners alight!

Part of our commitment was to supply the 11 Group aerobatic aircraft and crew for air displays throughout the summer. The pilot chosen was Flight Lieutenant Sandy Davis who was ebullient, and had the makings of a fine fighter pilot, if only he could be controlled. I flew with Sandy on one rehearsal and I don't think that I have ever been so frightened in an aeroplane. It started with a normal take-off until unstick, but he then held it down in full burner to 480 knots by the end of the runway before pulling into a 5 g rotation to a vertical climb. He then pulled inverted and rolled to level at 10,000 ft. From then on the display consisted of a series of high 'g' turns, rolls and flybys. The whole trip took ten minutes and used 9,000 lb of fuel!

In 1975 we had a three month detachment to Kinloss while the Leuchars runway was being resurfaced and we carried out our QRA commitment from there. During our farewell party someone suggested that we bomb the Kinloss Mess with lavatory paper on departure with the last four aircraft. It was thought that if the rolls were slashed with a razor blade and stowed in the flap housings of our Phantoms they would shred to confetti when released. That was the theory. We did not know if it would work but we decided to try it, so we cleaned the Officer's Mess out of lavatory paper and had the groundcrew do the necessary. Sandy Davis and I were in the lead aircraft and after take-off early on a Sunday morning and a sedate four-ship flypast, we asked for, and received, permission to make a low pass over the Mess. In line astern formation, at 400 yards spacing in turn, we lowered the flaps at the crucial moment. Breaking my neck to look out the back I could see nothing, but as the No. 4 overflew, Barry Mayner called to say, "There's bog paper everywhere!" Mission successful, we returned to Leuchars where I had a telephone call awaiting me from the C.O. of Kinloss, Group Captain

John Pack (ex fighters). He was delighted, but there were many officers critically short of toilet paper who were less than pleased. Kinloss got their revenge when, at the welcome home drinks party on the grass outside the squadron, we had a message that a Nimrod would be overflying the hangar. When it approached at about 400 feet it slowly opened its vast bomb bay doors. It did not drop anything but it surely frightened us!

Not long after, whilst I was on leave in the Highlands, the squadron was practising for the annual Battle of Britain 'At Home' display at Leuchars in September. Keith Beck was leading a four aircraft formation and decided to finish with a flypast and a 'Canadian Break' which entailed rolling the wrong way into the break (i.e. in a left-hand break, you roll right for 270 degrees), with the No. 4 breaking first under the others. I had never seen this done and, if I had been there, I would certainly have advised against it. Jack Hamill, the squadron QFI [Qualified Flying Instructor], and his navigator Tim Wright, were not too happy about the manoeuvre so Keith took the four-ship at medium level to practise up towards Kirriemuir. Somehow Jack lost it and when Tim realised what was happening he called "Eject!" in the nick of time. They were alright, but one F-4 (XV580) went down.

The year 1976 was a very good one for 43 Squadron which by now was commanded by Wing Commander (later Air Chief Marshal Sir) Roger Palin. We had lots of QRA scrambles which were very good for morale, particularly for our new crews who were allowed to get in on the action, once they were declared operational. We also started to do a lot of low level overland sorties intercepting Buccaneers and Jaguars over Sutherland and the Western Isles. It was the best flying that I was ever to experience, very taxing and flown over fantastic country against great opposition. By now the RAF was firmly in the chair as far as air defence of the Fleet was concerned and the first real test was to come in the Autumn exercise, when we were tasked with some very long over sea sorties with tanker support. From our point of view these were largely a waste of flying hours, often with as much as 3–4 hours transit time which was a complete waste of fuel. However their airships and lordships said that it was necessary to prove the system. The following year I was to record an intercept at longitude 21 degrees west, due south of Iceland and west of Brest which illustrates how far afield we went, all in an aircraft with no HF radio or INS equipment. To put it bluntly, there were times when we didn't know where we were and we couldn't ask anyone.

In October, flying with Mike Bell, a first tourist who was later to become a test pilot, I came closest to leaping out when we had a double generator failure (can't happen they said) on finals at dusk over Leuchars. The electrically powered systems (there was no battery) in the F-4K included the intercom, cockpit lights and the stability augmentation system. The stab augs served to damp down control inputs and acted in opposition to application of bank. Unfortunately we were turning hard left when the failure occurred and as the effect was to remove the opposing force to the bank input, we therefore entered a rapid roll to the inverted position at approximately 600 feet. Mike was superb, considering it all went very dark and very quiet. He checked the roll and recovered to the upright position, lit both afterburners and started a climb, then deployed the ram air turbine which gave us emergency power. Initially I had made up my mind that I was ejecting once the aircraft had gone through the inverted position, because there seemed little point in leaving at low level with the aircraft inverted. In the event I did not have to. We recovered one generator and landed very carefully.

The following month I flew with 'Gordie' Batt on a supersonic missile firing trial. Launched from a mother ship Canberra 40 miles away, the target was an AQM37 Stiletto drone flying at 40,000 ft at Mach 1.4. We were flying at 30,000 ft at Mach 1.2 as the backup aircraft when the primary firer called a malfunction and we had to take over. I had a good firing solution and we fired at 13 miles, right in the heart of the missile envelope. The Sparrow missile came off the front port missile well and appeared as a smoke trail climbing on the starboard side, scoring a direct hit on the contrailing target streaking towards us. It was awesome, taking place in just a few seconds, and was proof positive that these things did sometimes work.

There were two detachments of note in 1977, one to Bruggen for 'unlike' low level affiliation against the resident Jaguars and one to Keflavik in Iceland for a short exchange with the USAF Phantom squadron based there. We had seen them in the air several times when intercepting Soviet aircraft but had never sent any aircraft to Iceland before. We flew against them, 2 versus 2, allowing them their usual radar control and assistance, and were amazed at how incompetent they were. It transpired that the back-seaters had no radar training such as ours and simply acted as safety pilots, while the pilot did what the ground controller told him. We were, as usual, at pains to be totally unpredictable, sometimes splitting 10,000 ft vertical separation, and they simply had no answer. They would latch on to one of us and the other would simply creep up and have them both. We also provided two aircraft for the Royal Review flypast at Finningley, together with an airborne spare and a static display aircraft. This had top priority and, because of the many practices, mopped up an inordinate amount of effort. Roger and I flew one and, with the others managed to extract some training value by sending the airborne spare, if not required, up to the west coast of Scotland to act as a low level bounce for the returning pair. On the great day we flew on the right hand side of the lead Nimrod and we were heartily glad to wish goodbye to our big friend and pole off to the western isles for some low level combat.

Not long after, my tour came to an end and I found myself heading back to Germany. I can honestly say that my time on 43 Squadron was *phantastic* in every way. The squadron spirit, the ego boost of taxiing in with the canopy open and the seat up to the highest notch, and the sheer joy of being a fully paid up member of the finest is indescribable. It is therefore difficult not to look back on my tour on 43 as the high point in my service career. Long may the call of the Fighting Cock be heard in the land.

In the early days of Phantom operations the RAF was fortunate in being able to draw upon a large pool of highly experienced pilots and navigators who had learned their trade the hard way on much less sophisticated aircraft. One of those was Flight Lieutenant Guy Woods, a navigator whose initial radar training was completed on the Bristol Brigand prior to converting to the Meteor NF.12/14 and Venom NF.3 in the mid 1950s. He eventually joined 29 Squadron at Coningsby and here he describes a typical Phantom sortie.

A sortie of radar interceptions would normally last for about one and a half to two hours. However, the whole process including briefing, changing into kit, walking out, signing out, strapping in, starting up and getting airborne, flying the mission, returning, landing, taxiing back in and shutting down made the whole business last anything up to four hours. The first thing to do was to change into flying clothing. This meant stripping down to underpants and T-shirt and donning long johns and a cotton roll neck shirt. Next came the anti-g leggings, also delightfully known as ‘speed jeans’ or ‘turning trousers’. In the summer months a flying coverall went over everything but in the winter you donned a waterproof immersion suit for protection from the cold sea should you finish up in it following an ejection. In this case the overall was usually replaced by an acrylan pile 'Bunny suit' to provide the necessary insulation from the elements. Some thought the normal coverall would be all that was necessary under the immersion suit, but I took no chances! In later years the RAF joined the rest of the world's air forces and provided external g-suits which meant that, during the summer months, these could be left off until the last minute.

The lead crew normally conducted the briefing and this covered all aspects of the coming flight. First would come the weather, details of which included *en route* conditions, weather at base and alternates expected during the recovery phase, any strong winds such as jet streams, levels at which we could expect to generate contrails and anything else that might be considered significant. We would also be briefed on the air traffic situation locally and in general including any Royal Flights; certain protocols had to be observed when the Royals were out and about! Also included would be an intelligence briefing on the current threat to remind us what we would be up against. What to do in the event of an emergency was briefed and a specific in flight emergency situation would be discussed. Take-off, transit and recovery procedures would be covered in great detail so that by the time the briefing was over everybody knew exactly what they should be doing.

The next phase was to finish getting kitted up. In the early days this involved getting into the combined parachute/safety harness, but later on it was just a case of picking up and slipping on the lifesaving jacket. After this the crews would go to the operations desk where the pilots signed the authorisation sheet to signify that their crew knew what they were going to do and understood all the limitations which might affect the conduct of the sortie. The authorising officer would give a final update of anything else that might be significant and would round off with 'you are not cleared to crash'.... I jest!

After all the formalities had been completed the crews would walk out to their aircraft. On the way they would call in on the maintenance folk for a briefing on the state of their aircraft. This would include details of fuel carried, weapons on board, previous performance details of the radar and navigation equipment and any unserviceabilities being carried which would materially affect the flight. On arriving at the aircraft you would meet up with the groundcrew and brief them of anything unusual. The start-up procedure followed pretty much a set pattern and the crew chief was normally in contact with the flight crew on an intercom anyway. While the pilot did a walk-round external check of the aircraft, the navigator first checked the safety switches in his cockpit before climbing into the pilot's cockpit to check the safety of switches there. Once completed he would then switch the aircraft onto external power from a ground power unit and check the fuel booster pumps and switch on the radio.

Having satisfactorily completed these checks he would return to his cockpit and start aligning the inertial navigation system. This was the big delaying factor in the whole process of getting a Phantom in the air. A full alignment took 12½ minutes and one needed to get on with it without delay. Meanwhile the pilot would be getting on with his pre-flight checks, starting the engines and carrying out a variety of further checks to confirm the status of the flying controls and associated services. This was all done in conjunction with the crew chief, who would do a final walk round to confirm that all external supplies had been disconnected and that all hatches were closed and secure. Then we would be ready to go. The section leader would check in with the rest of the formation and request permission to taxi for take-off. Various other radio checks were completed at this stage to ensure that they were all working. When everyone was ready the formation would enter the duty runway ready for take-off. Sometimes we would take off as a pair in close formation, on other occasions we would do a stream take-off at 30 second intervals. Depending on the cloud structure you either stayed in close formation until on top, or followed each other using the radar.

Once on top the pair would split up into battle formation for the transit to the play area or, if in trail, practice closing in on each other using the radar to approach down to minimum radar range, simulating approaching a target for a night visual identification. This was a very important part of our training for the peacetime role and one that needed constant practice. The aim was to close in from a range in excess of one mile down to a range where the crew, especially the pilot, could see and identify the target which may be flying without its navigation lights. This is a potentially hazardous exercise and there have been many collisions over the years. Needless to say, the conduct of these visident runs is very carefully controlled by the authorities and the crews have to go through a whole series of practices before they are cleared to do them 'night, lights out' at all heights. Back in the bad old days we used to do these runs 'night, lights out' against evading targets, but not any more! These procedures were very much under the control of the navigator and we had to be very proficient at them. Once in the play area, somewhere out over the North Sea, we would get on with the main business of carrying out radar interceptions against each other. We would invariably be under the control of one of the main ground interception radar stations and would act as fighter turn and turn about with the other formation member.

The AWG-12 radar fitted to our F-4s was a marvellous piece of kit. It was a multi-mode radar with a pulse Doppler mode that gave it a superb 'look down' capability. When I began my career in air defence the bomber threat from the east was a high level one and a normal pulse radar was good enough against this sort of target. In the late sixties, however, the threat was deemed to be from bombers and attack aircraft operating at low level, so a look down capability was absolutely essential. There were a whole series of interception exercises we could carry out, each having its own code, and details of the sort of interceptions we would be carrying out would be passed to the Ground Controlled Interception (GCI) station before take-off.

Most of our work consisted of carrying out interceptions against low level targets. When acting as target you would fly at about 250 to 500 ft and any speed up to 500 knots for a normal target profile. There were two basic aims of an interception, either to identify the target, or to 'kill' it. The split and attack set-up between the fighter and target was very much under the control of the GCI. The target was given instructions in such a manner that the fighter did not know where it was in terms of heading, height and speed, but eventually the two of you would be approaching each other for the acquisition and attack phase. As you had asked and briefed for low level targets, you at least knew where to point the radar to see the target. The other piece of information you were given was the range of the target, apart from this you were on your own! You would eventually find the target and assess what it was doing in terms of heading, height and speed. For an attack, the aim was to position your fighter for a head-on shot using the Sky Flash missile and be in a good position to continue from there to a stern shot using the Sidewinder missile. These profiles were known as ARAs, short for Attacks/Re-attacks.

Although the UK had spent mega-bucks on the F-4, its one weakness as far as we navigators were concerned was the lack of a visor to put over the radar display to keep the sunlight out and there was certainly plenty of that when up in the air! The F-4 was delivered with a built-in overhead curtain under the rear canopy which could be pulled forward to cover the whole of the transparency and thus keep the sun out. I suppose the designers thought this would do and just left it at that. However, with the cover in place the navigator could not see out and the aircraft was short of a pair of eyes which, in combat, was not a good idea. Most navigators made their own visors using bits of rubber matting or similar, while others just bent right over the scope and excluded the light using their elbow. One of our engineers came up with a purpose built visor made of shaped rubber which fitted neatly onto the radar display and did the job admirably. The design was submitted for approval and was turned down by the authorities as being a loose article hazard. What do they know?! One copy of the visor was made into a pre-production model and this happened to fall into my hands. I enjoyed its use to the end of my days on the Phantom and still have it in my possession now. Of interest, the Tornado F.3 radar displays suffered even more badly than the F-4's in the sunlight and, you've got it, no visor was produced for the new aircraft.

We had it drilled into us from the very start that, before commencing an attack, you had to carry out the pre-attack checks religiously. The Americans lost innumerable 'kills' in south-east Asia during the Vietnam War through going into combat with the wrong, or no weapon switches made. So, even in training, we did the checks every time. This had disastrous consequences when one of our F-4 crews carried out an interception during an exercise in a QRA fit Phantom and fired off a live Sidewinder missile at a Jaguar which was shot down! (this incident occurred on 25 May 1982, the pilot of the Jaguar, Flight Lieutenant Steve Griggs, ejected safely). The other vitally important check was to set the front and rear cockpit altimeters to the same local pressure setting so that both instruments gave the same height above sea level. As a back-up the radar altimeter low height warning system was set appropriately. Of importance for the post-flight debriefing, a recording camera was switched on to record the radar display during the course of a radar attack. This reflected the old wartime mantra, 'no film, no kill'. It was just as important to switch the camera off again at the end of an attack, otherwise you would soon run out of film!

If the attack required you to descend to low level the crew were drilled to check height in the descent every 5,000 ft above 10,000 ft, and then every 1,000 ft below 10,000 ft. Despite these rules, crews still managed to fly into the sea with fatal results. We lost many crews over the years and, unfortunately, I am sure we will continue to do so for as long as we continue to fly. That sorted, the navigator would set the scanner depression angle, also known as tilt, so that you would pick up the target at the expected range. Having detected the target, the next thing was to assess what it was doing and set up the attack geometry. The initial moves were the same for both head-on and stern attacks. You had to manoeuvre your Phantom to place it on a parallel, head-on heading to the target, displaced five miles to one side or the other. If you were to carry out a 'kill' using the Sky Flash missile, at a pre-determined range you would turn onto a collision course with the target, as commanded by a steering dot under the pilot's control, lock the radar onto the target and launch the missile at the computed launch range. The geometry of this attack allowed a second bite of the cherry in that during the time of flight of the first missile you could manoeuvre your aircraft for a stern attack and use the Sidewinder as a back-up if the first attempt missed.

The initial moves for a stern attack were much the same, but instead of going onto a collision course, you continued in until it was time to commence a 180 degree turn in behind the target so as to roll out two miles behind. From there you could either manoeuvre for a Sidewinder shot, or continue for a visident. These profiles were pretty straightforward but could be complicated by target evasion, both in the head-on and stern phases of the attack. Interceptions required a high degree of crew co-operation and standardisation. Before the Phantom came along you would normally fly with your own pilot so you inevitably developed your own techniques, but in the days of the Phantom you seldom flew in a regular crew so standardisation was much more important. As a general rule during attacks, the navigator operated the radar and controlled the interception at long range, adjusting the geometry as required, while the pilot actually flew the aircraft, managed the weapon system and fired the missiles. The pilot had a repeater radar scope so could help out with interception geometry if necessary. Checks were a crew responsibility and aircraft safety certainly was. As an instructor I used to brief that the pilot would die a microsecond before the navigator unless you were hit from behind, so that it was vital that you looked out for each other!

These interception sorties were our bread and butter and there were many variations on the theme – high level subsonic and supersonic attacks, low level low speed attacks, medium level and so on. The Phantom was not a superb all rounder. It was not very good subsonic at high level. To do a stern approach on a high level target was quite tricky as it just would not turn satisfactorily at subsonic speeds. You had to do the long range approach to a high level subsonic target at a speed of at least Mach 1.2, only reducing to the target's speed when you were quite close in. For this type of interception we should have hung on to our Javelin FAW.9s!

With the practice interceptions completed it was time to go home. Hopefully there had been no deterioration in the base weather during our absence so we could make plans to recover there. If there was a bit of a transit we would fill the time in doing a tail chase or more practice visident runs – not a moment was wasted. Even basic battle formation needed practice – maintaining formation integrity while manoeuvring was an art in itself and needed constant practice. Recovery to base was usually pre-briefed depending on the weather expected. If the weather was good, a visual recovery was carried out as a pair of aircraft with a break into the circuit at 400 knots and 500 feet. Sometimes you would land from the first approach, but if sufficient fuel was available, circuits and bumps would be flown in different configurations.

If the weather was not so good you would come in, either as a pair or individually, to do an instrument approach. The navigator could use the radar to carry out what was known as an internal aids approach. All recovery and pre-landing checks were a crew responsibility and the important ones were carried out using a 'challenge and response' system. The navigator read out each check and didn't proceed to the next one before he had had the correct reply to the previous challenge. The same went for emergency drills. Each and every emergency situation had its own drill. The first and vital checks had to be known by heart by both crewmembers and were known as the **Bold Face Checks** because that was the way they were written! Follow up checks were carried out from the checklist. Many drills had many varied implications and to recover safely from a complex emergency required skilful handling and reading by the navigator and correct actions by the pilot.

Finally the aircraft was landed for the last time and taxied back into dispersal. Both crewmembers would have final checks to make and they would also have to make notes on equipment performance to debrief the maintenance people. On arrival at the parking slot more checks on aircraft systems were made before finally shutting down and vacating. The cockpits would be made safe in terms of ejection seat safety pins and switches and the aircraft would then be signed in at the flight line office where the tradesmen would be briefed on its performance. Next the crew would sign in from the sortie in the operations room and, having removed bulky safety equipment, retire to the crew room for a well earned cup of coffee prior to carrying out a post flight debrief. If the sortie had gone pretty much as planned this could be quite short, but sometimes if there had been complications or lessons to be learned, then the post flight deliberations could take a considerable amount of time.

29. The trials aircraft for the EMI recce pod was FGR.2 XV406 which is seen with the pod mounted on the centreline weapons station. *(Philip Jarrett)*

30. Close up of the EMI recce pod. It was used by 2 and 41 Squadrons at Laarbruch and Coningsby repectively for tactical reconnaissance until the units converted to the Jaguar in 1976/77. *(Philip Jarrett)*

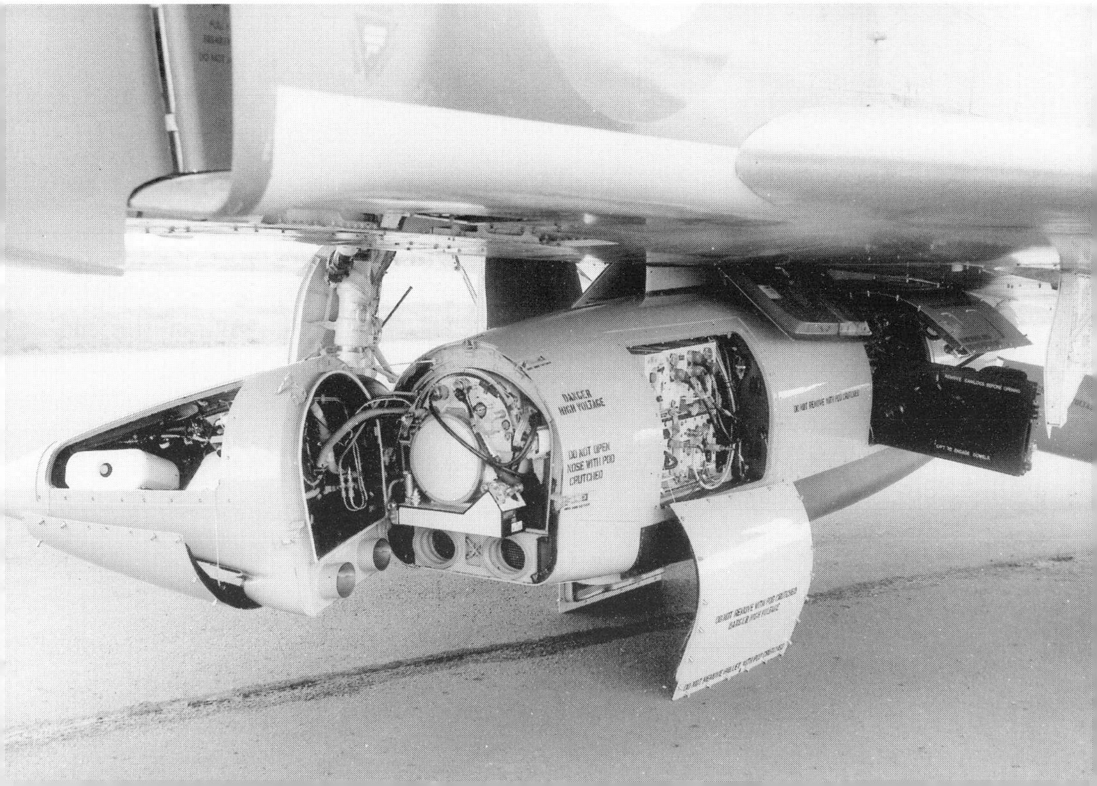

31. Camouflaged Phantom FG.1 XV583 of 111 Squadron revelling in the extra performance as a result of its clean configuration at Wyton in 1983. *(P. R. Caygill collection)*

32. Phantom FG.1 XV584 of 11 Squadron taxies out prior to displaying at Finningley in September 1983. *(P. R. Caygill collection)*

33. With its drag chute deployed, Phantom FGR.2 XV438 of 29 Squadron rolls to the end of the runway at Coningsby in June 1985. *(P. R. Caygill collection)*

34. Phantom FG.1 XV582 of 43 Squadron gets airbourne from Leuchars. *(Philip Jarrett)*

35. Phantom FGR.2 XT907 of 228 OCU photographed at Coningsby in March 1984. *(Philip Jarrett)*

36. Aggressively marked Phantom FGR.2 (XV500) of 56 Squadron carries a full load of Sparrow and Sidewinder AAMs and a SUU-23 gun pod. *(P. R. Caygill collection)*

37. Close up of the nose markings as applied to Phantom FG.1 XV569 of 111 Squadron pictured at Alconbury in 1986. *(P. R. Caygill collection)*

38. Phantom XV570 was one of the ex Royal Navy FG.1s transferred to the RAF when HMS *Ark Royal* was decommissioned in 1978 and flew with 111 Squadron. *(P. R. Caygill collection)*

39. FGR.2 XV498 of 17 Squadron shows off its SUU-23 gun pod during the Tactical Weapons Meet in June 1974. The six-barrel cannon was a potent weapon for close-in air-to-air combat but imposed significant performance penalties. *(Philip Jarrett)*

40. Phantom FGR.2 XT893 of 228 OCU. This aircraft was lost on 24 April 1989 when it crashed into the North Sea off Flamborough Head when flying with 56 Squadron. The crew ejected successfully *(P. R. Caygill collection)*

41. Phantom FGR.2 XV412 of 29 Squadron on the flight line at Coningsby in 1986.
(P. R. Caygill collection)

42. An unusual view of Phantom FG.1 XV587 of 43 Squadron with leading and trailing edge flaps extended.
(Philip Jarrett)

43. Phantom FGR.2 XT912 of 23 Squadron at low level. This aircraft survived until 14 April 1982 when it crashed after colliding with XT903 shortly after take-off from Coningsby when serving with 228 OCU. The crew ejected and XT903 landed safely. *(Philip Jarrett)*

44. Two Phantoms of 228 OCU taxi in after a sortie. *(P. R. Caygill collection)*

45. The nose and cockpit of Phantom FGR.2 XV424 of 56 Squadron marked up for Flt Lt Rick Offord (pilot) and Flt Lt Ian Wright (navigator). *(P. R. Caygill collection)*

46. Phantom FG.1 XV581 of 43 Squadron in the landing configuration. *(Philip Jarrett)*

47. One of the most widely travelled of RAF Phantoms, FGR.2 XV499 served with 6, 41, 92, 19, 23 and 29 Squadrons but is seen here in the markings of 228 OCU coded 'CF' in 1988. *(P. R. Caygill collection)*

48. A fully armed Phantom FGR.2 of 111 Squadron. *(Philip Jarrett)*

49. Phantom FGR.2 XT892 'CQ' of 228 OCU also carries the markings of 64 Squadron, the unit's reserve identity. *(P. R. Caygill collection)*

50. A long serving aircraft with 228 OCU, in whose colours it is seen at Finningley in 1988, FRG.2 XV393 subsequently flew with 74 Squadron in 1992 coded 'Q'. *(P. R. Caygill collection)*

51. Although it carries no squadron markings, Phantom FG.1 XT875 belonged to 43 Squadron and is pictured on the approach to Leeming in February 1989. *(P. R. Caygill collection)*

52. With the build up of the Tornado F.3 force at Coningsby, 228 OCU moved to Leuchars in 1987 where FGR.2 XT895 'CJ' is seen landing. *(P. R. Caygill collection)*

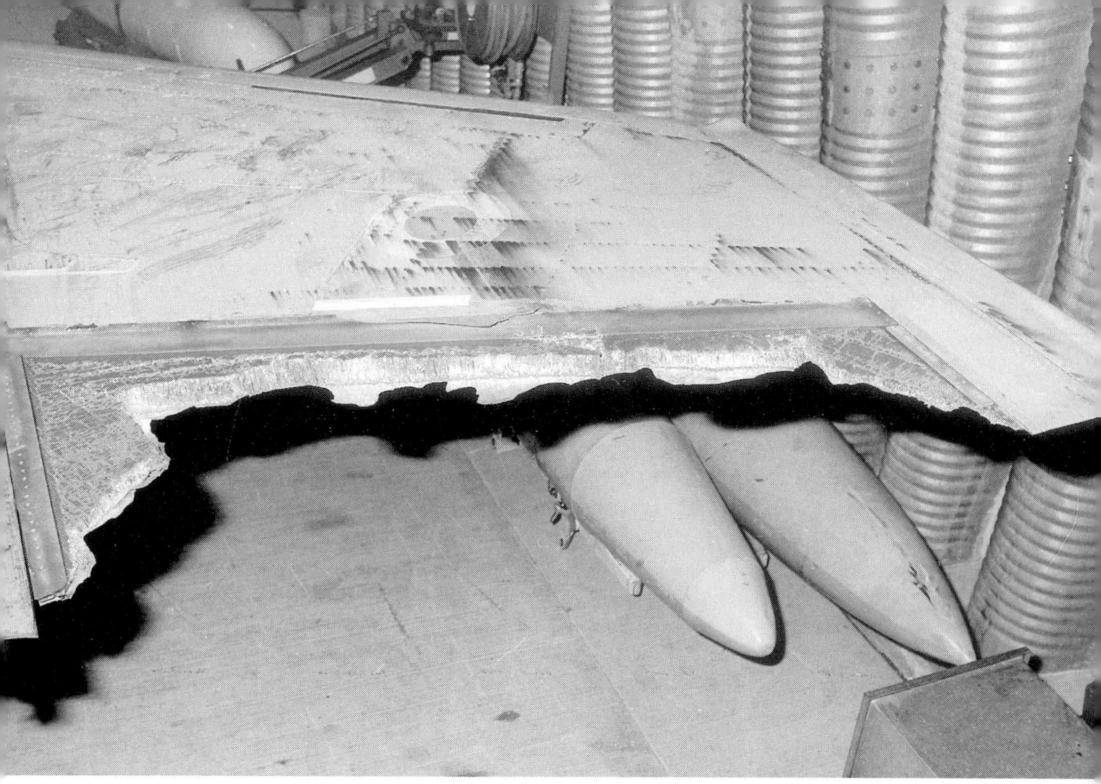

53. Damage to the outer starboard wing section of Phantom FGR.2 XV404 of 29 Squadron sustained during a sortie from Coningsby on 27 January 1987. *(Philip Jarrett)*

54. F-4J (UK) ZE351 'I' of 74 Squadron in happier times. It eventually became a hangar queen at Wattisham and ended its days on the fire dump at Finningley. *(P. R. Caygill collection)*

55. Phantom FG.1 XV577 'AM' of 43 Squadron seen taxiing at Finningley in 1986. *(P. R. Caygill collection)*

56. Phantom FG.1 XV582 'AF' of 43 Squadron cleans up after carrying out an overshoot at Linton on Ouse on 14 September 1988. This aircraft was later flown by 111 Squadron coded 'M' and was also used by 228 OCU. *(P. R. Caygill collection)*

57. In the last year of RAF Phantom operations, FGR.2 XV393 'Q' was painted in dual 56/74 Squadron markings and took part in numerous air shows in 1992. *(P. R. Caygill collection)*

58. Specially marked all blue Phantom FGR.2 XV408 of 92 Squadron seen at Leeming in 1992. A baggage pod had been fitted on the port Sidewinder rail. *(P. R. Caygill collection)*

59. The last 29 Squadron Phantom FGR.2 (XV412) overflies St Athan on 7 April 1987. *(Philip Jarrett)*

60. Stunning view of XV393, the last display Phantom, taken in July 1992. A long term resident of Coningsby with 228 OCU, this aircraft was one of fourteen such aircraft that replaced the F-4J (UK) with 74 Squadron in early 1991. *(Philip Jarrett)*

CHAPTER TWELVE

Crew Debrief – 2

Although the Lightning and Phantom were to fulfil similar roles with the RAF, their design philosophies were poles apart. Whereas the Lightning had been developed as the ultimate point defence bomber-destroyer, the Phantom was designed as a true multi-role combat aircraft capable of undertaking a wide range of missions from interceptor to low level ground attack, strike or reconnaissance. Having flown Lightning F.1s with 74 Squadron, Group Captain Mike Shaw subsequently had a long association with the Phantom and is well qualified to compare the two.

The Phantom, though better armed and with twice the fuel, was rather a disappointment after I had been spoilt by English Electric. Although the Lightning could not match the Phantom as a weapon, or in range or endurance, because it was lighter and aerodynamically cleaner, it handled very much better. I found the F-4B to be comparatively less refined as a flying machine. It had autostabilisation on all three axes (pitch, roll and yaw), all selected by a single magnetically-held switch, so a momentary interruption of electrical power could lead to a wild ride. Further, the roll channel would occasionally 'fight back', making a smooth roll impossible. Later F-4Bs had three separate locking switches so roll could be switched off. Pitch was always needed, particularly at aft CGs.

Pitch trim was also difficult because the stick position moved with trim. This meant that, as the F-4B accelerated, the pilot would find that he was trimming the stick further and further away from him. At high subsonic speed the pilot could not then rest his wrist on his knee, so the stick movement involved his whole arm. As one inch of stick movement could generate up to 6 g, this was not comfortable, and delicate pitch control was difficult. Worse, the cheap and nasty plastic stick-top had a circular force-transducer spring contact which allowed it to move about one eighth of an inch in any direction without effect on the flight controls. This made a Pilot Induced Oscillation (PIO) likely, when the pilot tried to damp out a pitch disturbance but would find that his arm had become an out-of-phase forcing function, making things worse. The Flight Manual for the F-4B stated that all high speed aircraft were prone to this – not the Lightning, or any other aircraft cleared by Boscombe Down.

When supersonic, the nose-down pitch change brought the Phantom's stick back within easy reach, as did the lowering of flaps. At these times the aircraft was delightful to fly, but in between, it needed a lot more development. Its turning performance, too, had been sacrificed to the God Mach 2, a speed hardly ever needed. The Phantom, except those fitted with leading edge slats, ran into pre-stall buffet whenever any serious back pressure was applied to the stick, although there was usually sufficient power from the responsive J79s to overcome drag. So, in combat manoeuvring, it was essential to keep speed and energy high and not to rely too much on turning performance, as the wings were too thin to provide much subsonic lift below about 450kts IAS. In the approach (dirty) configuration, the F-4B was above criticism and the Boundary Layer Control brought it in over 20 knots slower than the Lightning. To sum up, as a weapon system the Phantom was vastly superior, but as a pure flying machine the Lightning won every time.

Shortly after converting to the Phantom in 1969 'Bugs' Bendell had an opportunity to compare his new mount with his former favourite, the Lightning, during Number 6 Squadron's first Armament Practice Camp (APC) at Akrotiri in Cyprus.

On 7 October 1969 we laid on a simulated attack on RAF Akrotiri. The island was defended by the Lightning aircraft of No. 56 Squadron. Our attack was planned to take place at dusk. It was almost impossible to approach closer than 200 nautical miles to Cyprus and avoid radar detection, but we had one or two tactical surprises for the Lightnings. We flew outbound at high level in a single formation to a position some 250 nautical miles west of the island, before splitting into four independent pairs for a co-ordinated attack from widely differing sectors. We knew we would be detected, but we also knew the GCI controllers would have difficulty keeping track of our height, especially if it was constantly changing. The height profiles were left to the discretion of the pairs' leaders, although our simulated weapons load dictated that the final attacks would have to be mounted at low level.

The plan worked well; the Lightnings had to spread themselves thinly, and instead of flying in pairs they chose to operate as single aircraft, which was not the best tactic against a bomber force equipped with an effective counter-air capability. We were able to pick up the defending fighters at long range and, armed as we were with AIM-7E Sparrows, we could legitimately claim an effective air-to-air missile launch at fourteen nautical miles – far beyond the range of the Lightning's weapons. But in the nature of such exercises, old style, close-range dogfights between Phantoms and Lightnings were fought out some twenty miles west of Akrotiri. Compared to the Phantom the Lightning was superbly agile – although, had it been for real, few Lightnings would have survived to press home their attacks. Our planned strike on the airfield was delivered on time. At the subsequent debriefing the Lightning's claims and our counter-claims were hotly contested. We all learned a great deal from the experience but, in the end, there was little doubt that the Phantom was the superior aircraft.

With its multi-role capability, the Phantom replaced the Hunter FGA.9s which had been used to provide offensive support to No. 38 Group, Air Support Command, and also the Canberra B(I).8 low-level strike aircraft in RAF Germany. By the time that Flight Lieutenant Guy Woods converted as a Phantom navigator in the summer of 1969 he already had fourteen years experience including time on Venom NF.3s and Javelins, and two tours on Canberras flying low level reconnaissance with 31 Squadron in Germany and ECM training with 360 Squadron from Watton in Norfolk. After eight years out of a fighter cockpit he was looking forward to getting back into the world of Air Defence as he recalls.

I arrived at Coningsby in June 1969 to participate in No. 3 Course, the third course of aircrew for the newly re-forming ground attack squadrons, Nos. 6 and 54, which was due to top up the numbers of these two outfits. The first weeks were devoted to learning how to use the radar in the interception mode. Several of us navigators had been on Javelins previously and this stood us in good stead. However, it was not all easy going as the AWG-12 radar had an amazingly better performance than the old AI 17 of the Javelin and, very importantly, a look down mode provided by the pulse Doppler option of the radar. Our initiation was greatly assisted by a superb trainer made by the Goodyear Tyre Company! We all got through this phase successfully but some navigators came to grief on later courses and didn't complete their training. As an experienced navigator I, and one or two of my course mates, were able to give informal extra instruction in the 'black art' to those who were not so fortunate in their background (we were all at least second tourists at this stage but from various types of aircraft).

After the inevitable groundschool we eventually started the flying phase. My first sortie was a familiarisation trip with a staff pilot. This was terminated after twenty minutes following an engine failure – not an auspicious start! The flying course was split up into various phases. The first was the pilot conversion phase where the pilot went through a set of dual and solo exercises, i.e. with a QFI rather than a navigator before being deemed safe to continue the course as first pilot on type. For the flying phase I was crewed up with a young Hunter pilot by the name of Graham 'Black' Robertson who eventually retired from the RAF as an Air Marshal. Following completion of the conversion phase we tackled Air Defence. This consisted of about a dozen sorties of interceptions and half a dozen visual combat sorties (dog-fighting in other words, not a phrase particularly liked by the authorities!). Next came the Ground Attack phase, something I was not familiar with at all but my pilot was familiar with this type of attack from his Hunter days. This consisted of a variety of weapon deliveries including bombs, rockets and strafe using the SUU-23 gun pod. The final phase was Tactical Reconnaissance, where again I was back in my element having completed 3½ years in Germany doing recce, both at low and high levels. The Recce Pod was still a long way off so this was all done visually, with post flight verbal reports on targets reconnoitred being given.

My overall impressions of the Phantom, after some 47 hours on the beast, were what a fantastic piece of kit it was. It was big, powerful and truly awesome. It lacked some equipment, such as the Inertial Navigation and Attack System at first, but nevertheless it was really something. During the latter stages of training we learned of our future postings, it appeared that I was destined for No. 6 Squadron, however things took a different route. Peter Desmond was the specialist recce navigator at A&AEE Boscombe Down. He had been there several years and the RAF wanted him back! A replacement was needed to carry out the flight trials of the EMI Recce Pod, he needed to be recce experienced, familiar with the Javelin and trained on the Phantom. There weren't many of us about and I was selected for the job!

I arrived at Boscombe in January 1970 and during my time there we had a mixed bag of F-4s including two pre-production F-4Ks, a hybrid F-4K/M that had the airframe of a K and the avionics of the M, and several F-4Ms of which XV406 was the recce pod trials aircraft and fully instrumented for the job. One of the F-4Ks (XT598) was in service throughout my time at Boscombe, with and without radar, and we carried out a great variety of work on it, including XJ 521, the Sky Flash project. It was in XT598 that I flew in two memorable trips, both in the clean configuration. The first was a supersonic dash down the English Channel to see how fast it would actually go. This involved using the appropriate acceleration profile during which, if you moved your head to induce a bit of parallax on the combined speed instrument, you could kid yourself that you were doing Mach 2 but in truth the maximum speed we achieved on that sortie was Mach 1.98. The other was a maximum rate climb to 40,000 ft. I started the stopwatch at brakes-off, we accelerated in full burner to the appropriate speed then climbed like the legendary home sick angel. We bunted over the top to level at 40,000 ft in two minutes twelve seconds. Lightning pilots wouldn't be impressed but it was quite a ride!

The trials we carried out on the F-4 fleet included weapon carriage, release, aiming and jettison in every conceivable configuration, attitude, height and speed, and could be quite exciting. We did numerous weapon delivery and aiming trials on the range at West Freugh near Stranraer in Dumfries and Galloway. One of these involved carrying the maximum load of 1,000 lb bombs which precluded the use of underwing tanks and necessitated us landing at the airfield at West Freugh. To save a lot of trouble we planned to 'hot refuel' so we wouldn't have to shut down, turn round and go through the whole start-up rigmarole. There was a procedure, but the powers that be were reluctant to let us use it. We managed to persuade them and duly carried out the mission satisfactorily, however there was a slight hiccup in that the internal wing tanks filled asymmetrically, although there was no real way of knowing this. Needless to say one wing dropped markedly on take-off, frightening the pants off both of us.

Although I enjoyed the weapons trials, my *raison d'etre* at Boscombe was, of course, the recce pod. The flight trials programme seemed to go on for ever but, in fact, lasted from May 1970 to June 1971. During this period every aspect of the pod was examined in detail, including its effects on aircraft performance and the capabilities of all the various sensors, both optical and electronic. The trials progressed without any major incident although on one low-level, high-speed dash at 250 ft and 550 knots along a route that had been cleared for testing the TSR.2 we overflew a farm at which a farmer had been shoeing a horse. The noise of our passage frightened the horse more than somewhat and the farmer got kicked, nothing too serious, but word did get back to us!

My time at Boscombe Down came to an end and I returned to Coningsby in November 1974. I duly completed the last ground attack course on the OCU with a view to going on to No. 41 Squadron, the UK based recce outfit, however, I didn't really want to do that as the whole of the F-4 fleet was reverting to the Air Defence role in the near future and I wanted to get back to my roots. A friend took pity on me and arranged for me to go onto the OCU as an instructor on completing the course. Thus I was able, some fifteen years after graduating as a fighter combat leader on Javelins, to put those skills to good use on the F-4. The job of a navigator instructor on the OCU was to teach the new navs to use the interception modes of the radar. We did this both on the ground using the Goodyear AI trainer and practically in the air, where we showed to student pilots how it was done and watched the student navs doing their thing. The student navigators did a lot of their flying with staff pilots who contributed much to post flight debriefings.

Life on the OCU was pretty humdrum with courses coming and going at regular intervals although there were some interesting trips and a few hair-raising moments. One in particular involved the Queen's Silver Jubilee Flypast. This big formation duly overflew Buckingham Palace and continued at low level to fly over Strike Command Headquarters – all in the London Air Traffic Control Zone. Towards the latter stages of the flypast the weather began to deteriorate significantly and those of us at the tail end of the formation were forced lower and lower to the point where we finished up flying in and out of cloud over High Wycombe main street. Suddenly our aircraft was subjected to the most violent vibrations and I really thought we were flying through the tree tops. I was just psyching myself up to pull the black and yellow handle when my pilot screamed, "It's alright, it's just the slipstream of the Lightning in front." About this time our wingman, Steve Nichol, disappeared in cloud for the last time and left the formation, to be followed by all the other aircraft which used afterburner to climb as quickly as possible. I called up London Centre to tell them to be ready for a mass invasion of controlled airspace and we gladly allowed them to take over control. Fortunately, everyone survived this episode but it wasn't until we finally made it back to Coningsby that we could confirm that we were all safe. I've been on some major flypasts in my time, but that was the most frightening. Thank goodness for khaki underpants!

The routine was broken from time to time when we participated in major defence exercises as No. 64 Squadron which allowed us to experience life as lived on the regular squadrons. We took the occasional break from normal duties in order to run armament practice camps where we honed our gunnery skills and missile practice camps where we fired air-to-air missiles on the Aberporth range. In all my time in Air Defence I had not fired a missile at all. On my first occasion I was crewed with an ex F-4 recce pilot and we were tasked with doing a snap-up Sidewinder shot against a Jindivik target. Our first attempts were abortive, for some reason my pilot could not seem to aim the missile correctly and we returned to base without firing. A second sortie went the same way but on the third sortie I twigged what was going wrong and managed to control my pilot into a firing position. He duly released the missile and off it went into a steep climb to the target. By the time we fired, however, the towed flare and the Jindivik were exactly lined up with the missile's trajectory and the Sidewinder hit the Jindivik and destroyed it. The authorities were quite upset at the loss of another Jindi, but the sight was spectacular to say the least.

I continued on the OCU for 2½ years, after which I had had enough. The possibility of a posting back to Boscombe Down occurred and it was all but settled when someone in postings realised that I had been there before and, with a sense of fairness, allowed another navigator to go, although at the time I was somewhat miffed! Shortly after this a navigator on 29 Squadron was killed in a motorcycle accident and I applied for his post on the squadron. Accordingly I had the easiest posting in the world when I went from one hangar to another on a Monday morning to start what was to be my last flying tour. I didn't know how I was going to react to squadron life as I was nearly forty-three years old. In the event, I had a marvellous time on the squadron. We had a good variety of flying, comprising routine interception sorties (although the large diversity of profiles made them far from routine) and air-to-air refuelling with numerous detachments. There were squadron exchanges, trips to exotic locations, regular deployments to the Mediterranean, including Cyprus and Malta for gunnery practice and a host of other things to keep life interesting.

I initially crewed up with an old chum from my 25 Squadron Javelin days, one Keith McRobb. He was an outstanding pilot and showed me the ropes so that my transition to fully operational squadron navigator was both rapid and easy, and I was able to settle into the normal routine without difficulty. Subsequently I teamed up with two pilots on a fairly permanent basis and, in turn, showed them how it was done when they arrived fresh from OCU. They were Dick Fallis and John Botham, both of whom had experience in the role, but on different aircraft. They were both excellent pilots and were a joy to fly with. I finally crewed up with the squadron commanders, Wing Commander Tim Elworthy and Wing Commander Ian MacFadyen in turn to finish off my time with the squadron.

By the late 1970s a feature of our training was Dissimilar Air Combat with the USAF Aggressor Squadron based at RAF Alconbury. This outfit flew Northrop F-5 fighters and were painted up to look like Soviet Air Force fighters. The tactics they used in close combat were based on Soviet systems and the aim was to train us to cope with this particular threat. Accordingly, we detached to Alconbury for a period of a week or so and took part in their course. The academic work was interesting to say the least and the flying was outstanding. The after duty hospitality was excellent as well! I recall during one sortie that one of the F-5s flew through our slipstream and such was the buffeting it took that the fin and rudder assembly was severely buckled and it had to divert to Coningsby in a hurry. That was certainly a novel method to get a 'Bogey' off your 'Six'.

A regular feature of life on the squadron was the deployment to the Mediterranean for an Armament Practice Camp. Initially these were held in Malta but eventually the RAF facility had to be closed as a result of political pressure and future camps were held at Akrotiri in Cyprus. The whole squadron, including ground crew and other support staff, were deployed and the aircraft flown out with air-to-air refuelling. These long transit sorties could be quite a bore, the tankers did all the navigation and all we had to do was plug in at the appropriate time. Our navigators were expected to keep a normal log and chart of the navigation situation *en route* and this did a lot to relieve the monotony. It was on one of these deployments that a hilarious bit of R/T occurred. Athens Control was trying to contact a British Airways Speedbird aircraft. Our flight commander who was leading our four-ship relayed the message. His navigator, whose mind must have been elsewhere at the time, heard this transmission and thinking it came from 'Speedbird XYZ' replied. His pilot up front had similar thoughts and the conversation between the two cockpits went on for some time before it finally dawned on them that neither Athens Control nor 'Speedbird XYZ' was in the loop!

These detachments lasted five or six weeks and allowed the whole squadron to get to know itself thoroughly. The first half was devoted to air-to-air gunnery using the SUU gun pod against a towed banner until all pilots had demonstrated a satisfactory hit rate. There were some amazing scores achieved with this system, unlike those of the old night-fighters where 10 or 15 per cent might be considered a good result. Scores of 50 per cent or more were regularly achieved and, I believe, the odd 100 per cent was scored. In earlier days the navigator had little to do with gunnery apart from locking the radar onto the banner as with the Javelin, whereas with the F-4 he had to help set up the attack using the radar, then lock the radar onto the target, while being subject to very high roll rates and lots of positive and negative 'g'. It was all quite physically exhausting and if you could keep hold of your breakfast you were certainly proved immune from motion sickness!

During one of my returns to the UK after a Cyprus detachment we had an anxious moment. I was in the lead four with a tanker and flying with Tim Elworthy. Gus Hay and Geoff Day were in one of the F-4s when about forty-five minutes out from Akrotiri they suffered a utilities hydraulic failure that necessitated them breaking off and returning to Cyprus. They duly left the formation and we continued on our way. Shortly afterwards I heard a very faint 'Mayday' over the radio from the stricken Phantom. Tim didn't hear it at first but did the second time. Gus informed us that he had experienced an engine failure and was trying to make it back to Akrotiri. Tim decided that he needed help so we turned round and 'hot footed' our way back east.

We remained in radio contact and Gus told us that the weather at low level was not at all good with poor visibility and severe thunderstorms, typical of the Med in mid December. I busied myself with the radar trying to pick out one small bright dot from the rest of the clutter. Tacan air-to-air ranging showed us how far away Gus and Geoff were and the reducing range showed that we were going in the right direction. Their navigation system was unserviceable so they had very little idea of precisely where they were. I eventually picked up the F-4 and we were able to join up with it and escort it back to Akrotiri where we both landed safely. Fortunately, the ground crews and spares back-up had not yet departed and, as luck would have it, a Victor tanker was still on the ground. The Phantom needed a replacement engine which was fitted in record time and an air test carried out with satisfactory results. Strike Command agreed to hold the tanker until we were ready to go and after a delay of four days we were able to resume our journey home to arrive back in the UK just before Christmas.

Another detachment I was able to enjoy was the trip to Iceland to operate with the USAF 56th Fighter Interception Squadron who guarded that part of the North Atlantic. Our squadron commanders were very reluctant to let us do this deployment because, due to the usually inclement weather, the chances of doing much flying while there were remote to say the least. What the Bosses usually did was to announce the evening before departure that this deployment was on in the hope that it would be too late to organise the two crews required. I and three others were able to call their bluff twice but of course the Bosses were absolutely right. For the first detachment the weather was good enough for us to get in and out of Iceland, but the interval between arrival and departure was so bad that flight operations were impossible. The second trip was similarly non-productive because the Icelandic government would not allow the scheduled exercise to take place. However, the American hospitality was its excellent self and we had a good time. When we did manage some flying we did some 'unlike' combat against the 56th FIS T-33 ECM training aircraft which allowed us to put into practice the skills we had learned with the Aggressors.

One of the nice things about the navigator's cockpit in the Phantom was the instrument panel, the cluster of instruments of which would not have looked out of place in the pilot's cockpit of older fighters. I particularly liked the provision of an Artificial Horizon which was to stand me in good stead one evening at dusk. I was flying with one of our young pilots on his first sortie after having ejected on the runway the previous week. We had completed a handling sortie and were back in the circuit. The cloud base was marginal for visual circuits and as we completed our initial approach we were asked to go round again to let another aircraft get off. We flew along the dead side at a thousand feet in and out of cloud and as we passed the take-off end of the runway, the pilot put on 90 plus degrees of bank to watch the other aircraft on its take-off run. Just at that moment we popped into the bottom of the cloud with a lot of bank on. There was a deathly silence from the front cockpit and I realised the pilot had fallen into the unusual position trap and hadn't got much idea which way was up. Fortunately, I was able to use my Artificial Horizon and command him "Roll Left, Roll Left" until the wings were more or less level. We popped back out of cloud in quite a steep attitude from which he was able to recover, but the incident certainly set the old heart racing!

After finishing his tour on 29 Squadron, Guy Woods remained in Air Defence and helped to introduce the Tornado F.2/F.3 to RAF service by instructing navigators on interception techniques using the aircraft's Foxhunter radar. On leaving the RAF he became a civilian groundschool/ simulator instructor at 229 OCU Coningsby. Despite the sophistication of modern radars, he found that the techniques he had been taught back in 1955 still held good, although he recalls that the vastly increased detection ranges allowed navigators more time to sort out the cock-ups made by the ground controllers!

Having begun his flying career on Chipmunks at the Primary Flying School, South Cerney and Jet Provosts at 3 FTS Leeming, Group Captain Graham Clarke went on to amass nearly 2,400 hours in Lightnings during spells with 11 (twice), 19 and 29 Squadrons and the Lightning Training Flight before he converted to the Phantom in 1979. He went on to fly with 92 Squadron, part of 2ATAF in Germany and was to have the honour of commanding 74 'Tiger' Squadron at Wattisham for nearly three years.

Coming from a Lightning background I found the stick and engine controls on the Phantom to be a good deal heavier, but on the plus side it had lots of fuel, good weapons and a superb radar. The Phantom was manoeuvred with reference to an angle of attack gauge, get it wrong and you were soon into deep buffet with the speed falling away rapidly. One thing that soon became apparent was that the tyres just seemed to keep on going which was in marked contrast with the Lightning, one landing in anything like a decent crosswind and they were shot!

My first trip in a Phantom was on 2 February 1979 in XT894 at 228 OCU, Coningsby. As I had plenty of fast jet experience I took the short course which involved general handling, instrument work and air combat training in 1 versus 1 and 1 versus 2 situations. After completing the course I was posted to 92 Squadron at Wildenrath in RAF Germany. It was here that I took part in a BBC documentary which went out in the Man Alive series. The programme looked at how Wildenrath coped with NATO exercise *Cloudy Chorus* and involved interviews with a number of crew members, myself included. My chief recollection however, is of Jack Pizzey, the BBC reporter I flew in the back seat of a Phantom, being continually air sick!

We flew yearly Armament Practice Camps at Akrotiri. The flag we used was only 24 ft long by 6 ft wide but when you approached it at an angle it looked a lot smaller and appeared almost square. Unlike the Aden gun on the Lightning, the SUU gun pod was not subject to stoppages and fired at the prodigious rate of 100 rounds per second. The target was towed by a Canberra at 180 knots and we approached at 380 knots. I always seemed to manage an above average rating for air-to-air gunnery and later in my career I achieved a score of 62.9 per cent in an F-4J. One of the best aids to gunnery was the so-called 'yaw string' which was a piece of cord fixed to the outside of the windscreen, keep it straight and you had perfect directional trim. Our training also involved dissimilar air combat against a wide variety of types ranging from Harriers, Jaguars and F-104 Starfighters, to the Nimrod maritime reconnaissance aircraft. Harriers were difficult opponents but Jaguars were relatively easy as they lacked power and didn't turn particularly well. The Nimrod could be surprisingly tricky as it could turn tightly, put out flares and chaff and had plenty of onboard systems to bugger our radars.

My final operational tour was as O.C. 74 Squadron on the F-4J. Compared to the FGR.2, the feel of the J was much lighter, not quite in the same league as the Lightning, but not far off and much better than the Spey Phantom. As Phantoms were needed for the Falklands detachment we practiced airborne refuelling with C-130 Hercules which was an interesting experience. The 'Herc' flew much slower than the VC 10 and Tristar tankers we were used to but, unlike the Tornado F.3, the Phantom could cope quite easily, to slow down you just pulled back on the stick and banged on some power. Towards the end of the Phantom we got the chance to fire more Sparrow missiles than normal. Not all went as planned. One went 'loopy' and went straight up after launch causing all aircraft in the vicinity to scatter like mad, as what goes up will eventually come down again. Going back to my first Phantom tour I had actually managed to shoot down one of the Jindivik drones which didn't go down too well. Whenever they lost one it was always claimed that the one you had shot down was the best one they had!

During my two tours on Phantoms I had very few incidents, an engine failure on take-off in an FGR.2 and the occasional hydraulics failure. One of the more unusual incidents occurred to one of the FGR.2s that replaced the F-4Js on 74 Squadron in early 1991. It suffered de-lamination of the nose radome which came off in a long helical strip at 600 knots and 250 ft. The material was ingested by the engines but fortunately no serious damage was done and the aircraft landed safely. My tour as boss of 74 Squadron was one of the most enjoyable of my career and when it finally came to an end I had over 1,400 hours on Phantoms. Although the Phantom could not compare with the Lightning as a pilot's aeroplane, I still look back on it with great affection as it did everything that was asked of it and very rarely let me down.

Chapter Thirteen

Phantom Test Pilot

Throughout its life with the RAF and Fleet Air Arm the British version of the Phantom was the responsibility of Hawker Siddeley Aviation (later British Aerospace) at its base at Brough near Hull, with all flight testing being carried out at Holme-on-Spalding Moor, a former 4 Group bomber base which had been taken over by Blackburn Aircraft in 1957 from the USAF. All modifications to the Phantom fleet had to be cleared by HSA/BAe before service use and the company was also heavily involved in resolving some of the problems that occurred during its career.

Don Headley was one of those who carried out testing work on the Phantom, latterly as BAe's Chief Test Pilot (CTP). As a raw nineteen-year-old he joined No. 14 Squadron at Fassberg in Germany in 1952, with whom he flew Vampire FB.5s and Venom FB.1s, before transferring to night/all-weather fighters with 64 Squadron, initially on the Meteor NF.12/14 and subsequently Javelin FAW.7/9s. After leaving the RAF in 1962 he spent five years ferrying a wide variety of Royal Navy aircraft for the RN Civilian Ferry Flight which was run by Short Brothers, before joining Hawker Siddeley in 1967 to take up testing duties on the Buccaneer low level strike aircraft and the F-4. He recalls his introduction to the Phantom.

> The first flying for Hawker Siddeley was done by Derek Whitehead and J. G. 'Bobby' Burns who both went to the USA to do a conversion course with McDonnell Douglas. They then came back, but eventually Bobby left and I was asked to convert to the Phantom which I did with the RAF at 228 OCU Coningsby. My initiation to the Phantom was overseen by Arthur Vine, a rather 'aged' instructor whose son was a captain on Shackletons, something that we found

> rather amusing with his Dad still on fast jets! My first flight was on 14 May 1973 in XT906 and on returning someone asked me what I thought of the aeroplane. I replied that my immediate impression was that it had been designed for long-legged, long-armed, dim Texans because the dashboard was further away than on British aeroplanes, the stick was long and nowhere near the pilot, it had a big throttle and the undercarriage control consisted of an oversized lever with a large red plastic wheel that also had a light in it. I was unable to think of a reason why the designer felt it necessary to incorporate the latter, unless he had a very low regard for the intelligence levels of the pilots who would fly his creation. My conversion consisted of four flights plus simulator work, and took in general handling, circuits, supersonic handling and single-engine circuits. One nice aspect of the Phantom was that it did not have too much of an asymmetric problem when flying with one engine shut down. As the engines were mounted so close together the disturbance directionally was hardly noticeable.

The work carried out at Holme-on-Spalding Moor comprised anything from relatively mundane production testing, to trials to clear the Phantom at the extremes of its performance envelope. Shortly after converting to the Phantom Don Headley was involved in a programme to measure wing fatigue, one that required maximum rate turns to be carried out at supersonic speeds over the North Sea.

> The testing we did varied tremendously and one of the first things we had to do was a wing fatigue trial because fitting the Spey engines had altered the structure around the centre section. We had three development aeroplanes which were fitted with strain gauges and we then went up to do the usual fatigue trials involving accelerating to high speed and applying high 'g' loadings, at various Mach numbers. It all culminated in the hardest bit which was supersonic at 1,000 ft – the engineer's were always keen for us to do the testing at sea level as it made their calculations easier. We had to fly off the coast but at 1,000 ft we were too low for the radar to give us any clearance, so it had to be visual clearance to keep clear of shipping and so on. We could only do the speed runs in the clean configuration without wing tanks and as we had to be in full reheat we were fairly limited on fuel. Once we were supersonic at about 1.2 M at low level, we went into a turn which was gradually increased until 6 g was applied which was the limit at supersonic speeds in the Phantom as the stick was on the back stop at this point. As speed reduced you had to remember to

move the stick forward when subsonic because if the stick was held fully back the aeroplane would tend to 'dig in' and exceed the 'g' limit as the Centre of Pressure altered. It certainly felt very, very fast at 1,000 ft at close to 1,000 mph.

The only way to maintain speed at 6 g was to do a wind-up turn where you would let the nose drop. This was done at 20,000 ft over the sea. At altitude we were getting 1.7–1.75 M so in my experience at least the Phantom was not a Mach 2 aeroplane. It could well be that the American version with General Electric engines could get there if the pilot unloaded the aeroplane, but the British Phantom certainly could not, unless the conditions were particularly favourable. Each flight only lasted about thirty minutes or so and the fuel low level light was invariably on during the return to Holme-on-Spalding Moor. This series of tests were particularly arduous, but were exhilarating nevertheless.

In keeping with its remit as a multi-role fighter, the Phantom had the ability to carry a wide variety of external stores and when fully loaded it weighing in at 58,000 lb, or slightly more than three Hunter FGA.9s at maximum weight. Don Headley was tasked with clearing the take-off and landing characteristics of the Phantom in this condition, the trials being carried out at RAE Bedford.

I did the emergency heavyweight landing clearance on the Phantom that the RAF wanted in case of an engine fire immediately after take-off. Incidentally the original Phantom did not have any fire extinguishers fitted, unlike the British version, so the Americans were obviously relying on Mr Bang seat! We went down to Bedford to use their long runway and also because they had a deck landing mirror that we were able to set up to assist me to achieve the correct rate of descent. On the downwind leg the procedure was for me to call out my fuel state so that those on the ground could calculate total weight and give me the angle at which I had to come in to hit the deck at around 18 ft/sec. Having done that with both engines, we had to repeat the exercise on one to simulate an engine fire, and eventually I went down to Cyprus to declare it for hot weather conditions. The problem there was that with full flap on one engine and in twelfth stage blow, to get the lowest landing speed, you needed reheat to keep to the correct approach speed. If you didn't, you had to land with half flap which, depending on runway length, could be a bit tight. Then again, if the Phantom had been single-engined, the pilot would not have had any choice in the matter!

The heavyweight landings all came to grief in XT596 when I had a tyre burst on take-off and we went off the side of the runway. This was another case where you had to be careful on flight testing because when this trial was originally planned, I looked at the flight test schedule and they had used fuel tanks to get up to the maximum weight. Some of the most dangerous flight testing you can do is to check landing performance where you are using maximum rate braking at the maximum allowable brake speed. The technique was to lower the nosewheel and as soon as the correct speed was achieved to apply full brake and hold it on. Under such conditions it would be very easy to suffer a burst tyre so I informed them that I wouldn't do it with fuel and suggested that we do it with 'dead' bombs instead. This was agreed which, in the end, was just as well.

The big problem was tyre temperature and at maximum weight the aeroplane was not becoming airborne until 150–160 knots had been achieved which was very close to the tyre limiting speed. The occasion when I crashed on take-off was the second sortie of the day and we checked tyre temperature before taxiing which, at the time, was within limits. However, we had a long way to taxi and Air Traffic stopped us three times. This built up the tyre temperature which was exacerbated by a characteristic of the Phantom to run away from you when idling and this meant that you had to frequently apply brake against power. I believe that when I eventually started the take-off run, the temperature was already too high and the tyre burst at around 110 knots. We left the runway at 85–90 knots but unfortunately there was a concrete camera mount flush with the grass and the left wheel hit that which swung us round and put the wheel up through the wing. We eventually came to rest with 'dead' bombs everywhere. Although it would have been feasible to do so, it never crossed my mind to eject, although if my background had been Navy instead of RAF I would have been out! That stopped the trial but we had done enough by that stage to clear the Phantom for service. The aeroplane was initially classified Cat 5 which was a write off, but it was later transported back to Holme-on-Spalding Moor and repaired, and in fact my very last flight in a Phantom on 30 September 1982 was in XT596 (this aircraft was the second YF-4K and was used exclusively on trials work before being delivered for display at the Fleet Air Arm Museum at Yeovilton on 19 January 1988).

Any major problems encountered with the Phantom in service were referred back to HSA/BAe for rectification work to be carried out. Don Headley recalls some of the snags that were encountered and another instance where he had to put his foot down with those in charge of flight testing.

> We had something that was known as 'biscuit tin lidding' on the fuselage fuel tanks that flexed in service like a biscuit-tin lid with the result that fatigue cracks were developing. All the aeroplanes were returned to HSA/BAe in sequence for modifications which was quite a big job as it involved the whole of the top of the fuselage. The other regular task that we had to do was repair work to the tailplane skinning. The undersurface of the tailplane was made of titanium which tended to crack badly over a period of time due to excessive heat and shock waves when the engines were operated in reheat.
>
> Everything that flew on the Phantom had to be cleared by us from a structural and aerodynamic handling point of view before it could be used in service. I was asked to do the firing trials on the SUU-23 gun pod and this was another case of being asked to do something that I initially refused to do because they were asking me to fire the gun when supersonic in a climb. The range we were using was over the sea, off Boulmer in Northumberland, and once again it had to be visual clearance as the area could not be cleared of shipping. I tried to get some reassurance as regards bullet trajectory, as an aeroplane had managed to shoot itself down when supersonic after descending to a lower level, having overtaken the shells which then dropped on to it. I wasn't happy, especially as I would have the added responsibility of clearing the range myself as well, so I said, "I'm not doing it" to which they responded by saying, "You can't say that!" The whole situation was eventually resolved, but occasionally in test flying the technical people do ask you to do things without realising the implications.

Although the flying at Holme-on-Spalding Moor was often routine, those involved in testing the Phantom could not be sure what they would be faced with from one day to the next. In late 1976 an unusual request came in from the RAF, asking whether it would be possible to land a Phantom successfully with the outer wing detached. This came about following the loss of XV417 of 29 Squadron which suffered failure of the starboard wing tip on 23 July 1976 during Air Combat Training over the North Sea. Although the pilot managed to regain control of the aircraft, the crew were forced to eject off the Lincolnshire coast. Don Headley was given the job of finding out if a Phantom could be recovered with part of the wing missing.

After the starboard wing tip came off a Phantom when in combat with F-5s off the Dutch islands, the Board of Inquiry looking into the accident asked us if it would be possible to land a Phantom with the outer wing missing. We said that we didn't really know, but that it might be possible to do a trial in the simulator. Our technical people at Brough put their heads together and very cleverly came up with a way to tell the simulator that part of the wing wasn't there any more. This was not easy as we had to replicate the combat conditions exactly in terms of overall weight. We then simulated the wing off situation by loading that side with enough weight to equal the loss of lift on that wing. Having done that, however, we needed to increase drag on the port wing, because, with part of the starboard wing missing there was reduced drag on that side. Once all the simulator software had been set up I went down to fly it.

I flew the sortie exactly as it had been recorded in the pilot's report and took the aeroplane up to 17,000 ft. I asked them not to tell me when they intended to pull the switch to simulate the wing failure, but when they did I went into a spiral and crashed in the sea! The second time, as I did not have God's big horizon to help me, I got them to give me a bit of a warning. On this occasion I went into a spiral but recovered by 5,000 ft in exactly the same parameters as the pilot had indicated in his report. I then flew the simulator, as he had flown the aeroplane back to the coast off Coningsby, with a lot of crossed controls. In the actual incident, the pilot had been asked to do a low speed handling check, so he dropped half flap which put the aeroplane in seventh stage blow and reduced speed to the datum figure. It was then suggested that he lower full flap which turned out to be a fatal mistake, because when you put full flap down, you also drop leading edge droop which is on the outer wings as well. As soon as that was selected all the hydraulic oil went out through the hole where the wing wasn't! Once the oil was lost, that meant that the utilities system was gone which put the rudder into manual and so on, the aeroplane soon becoming uncontrollable.

We did all this on the simulator and eventually I wrote a report which suggested that you could put a Phantom down with the outer wing off provided, of course, that you only used half flap and landed at a minimum speed of 220 knots on a runway of at least 3,000 metres. One of the other problems was that having touched down at that speed you could not use the drag chute at first because you were way above the parachute weak link speed. You would, therefore, have to wait for the speed to drop off before the parachute could be deployed and you would also have to wait for speed to diminish before using the brakes. As speed over the threshold was also above the arrester gear limit, the only chance of an arrested landing was by using the gear at the far end of the runway. After deliberating long and hard, my answer to the President of the Board of Inquiry was, yes, it could be done, assuming the aeroplane was close enough to a suitable airfield, but I would strongly urge that no pilot be brought to task for deciding not to do it, for I knew what the RAF was like at that time as they would do almost anything to blame the pilot!

As a two-seat aircraft, the workload on the Phantom could at least be shared between the two cockpits during test flights, however, the role of the back-seater was far from easy, especially when engaged on performance testing. Don Headley recalls their role and some of the other flying that he had to undertake.

To begin with the chap in the back seat was usually a flight test engineer whose job it was to run through what we had to do and to monitor and make notes on what was happening. They really suffered, especially when we were doing the high-g trials, and I admired them a lot. Their flying pay was a pittance but when they came under me as Chief Test Pilot we managed to get them better remuneration. We eventually ended up with just two. I asked Jim Nottingham, an ex Phantom navigator from Coningsby, to come and join me as we needed someone who knew the radar inside out and he became my primary flight test navigator. The other was Mike Nicholl who had been one of the original flight test observers, so between them we had an extremely good team.

We were involved with all sorts of trials to clear equipment for the RAF including the AIM-9L Sidewinder and Sky Flash air-to-air missiles. We even had to test a new Nuclear/Biological/Chemical (NBC) suit and on this occasion I had a service navigator, Flight Lieutenant North, in the back fully dressed up. I refused to wear the suit and told them point blank that they had service test pilots who should be doing that sort of work! In January 1981 we went out with the Phantom to do the trial on the fully instrumented Air Combat Manoeuvring range in the Mediterranean off Decimomannu. The British Phantom had to be re-engineered to quite a large extent so it could transmit to the buoy in the sea, or the 'bueee' as the Americans, who were also out there, called it. I did that with Jim Nottingham in the back as he could use the radar, and we hauled it round to all the limits, changed the internals a bit, and then did a bit more. Eventually the RAF had clearance to use the range, the whole idea of which was that the instrumentation recorded everything for subsequent debrief. It was a great success – not the least because Squadron and Flight commanders could no longer get away with saying they had won when they hadn't!

Further tests included radio trials with the Rapier surface-to-air missile system and a new type of IFF. This was a highly secret trial which was called Exercise Braid. This new piece of kit worked on a coded system which, of course, had to be kept under wraps, as the last thing we wanted was for the 'enemy' to find out the method we were using. It was so 'hush-hush' that we were not allowed to mention the airfield we were to use. The whole thing nearly came to a premature halt when Jack Pearson, who was running flight test at that time, put out a memo that happened to mention that he had booked accommodation for everyone at a hotel in Woodhall Spa which did not leave anyone in any doubt as to which airfield we would be using! Because of that the Air Ministry very nearly cancelled the trial and moved it somewhere else. We were taking-off in the middle of the night and the people in the hotel couldn't make out what we were doing as we were coming in at 3 or 4 in the morning. The flying had to be carried out at that time as the trial involved jamming the national radar system, so we flew when there was the least civil traffic around.

In all Don Headley flew 429 hours on the Phantom during his time at HSA/BAe. Although he does not regard it as his favourite aircraft he was certainly appreciative of its performance, especially in the clean configuration, its prodigious load-carrying ability and multi-role capability. He sums up its qualities:

Although I flew around 1,500 hours on the Buccaneer and Phantom, neither could be regarded as my favourite. From a pure flying point of view nothing could compare with a single-seat Hunter. Once you graduated onto aeroplanes such as the Phantom, however, you were immediately aware of how complicated they were, although it was nice to have all that power! It used to amuse me when I was driving in to work; people would come tearing past me in the car and I would sit back and grin and carry on at a steady 50 mph or so, knowing full well that in an hour's time I would be doing 1,000 mph.

The acceleration on a Phantom in full reheat was always impressive. You could be doing 400 knots shortly after the end of the runway and, if you weren't careful, even going supersonic in the climb if the aeroplane was clean. To avoid this you had to keep pulling the nose higher and higher so as not to plant a sonic boom

> over land. There was a big difference when carrying underwing fuel tanks however, which, even if they were not full, would tend to spoil things by creating a lot of drag. The Phantom was also extremely good for aerobatics and you didn't have to worry too much about spinning it, unlike the Buccaneer which you did not spin. If you did, you ejected pretty quickly as it did not recover. The RAF lost a few Phantoms during aerobatics with pilots not pulling out in time, but that is always a problem with slippery aeroplanes. You could haul back on the stick and pull high 'g' to hold the speed back when pulling through a vertical manoeuvre, but you certainly did not want to be under 8,000 ft when at the top of a loop. When I demonstrated the Phantom I did not include loops in my routine, I never really saw the point as you would virtually disappear from sight, so I always concentrated on manoeuvres at a lower level which kept the aeroplane in view of the crowd.

After leaving British Aerospace, Don Headley continued to be involved in the world of test flying as Chief Test Pilot with Slingsby Aviation at Kirkbymoorside where he became heavily involved with the development of the T.67M Firefly single-engined basic trainer. At the time of writing the Firefly is in service in twelve countries throughout the world for *ab initio* instruction, which includes training military pilots destined for the RAF, USAF, the Royal Jordanian Air Force and the Bahraini Air Force. Although Don is now semi-retired, he continues to fulfil the duties of CTP at Slingsby on a part time basis.

Chapter Fourteen

Phantom Flight

For most air-minded civilians the chance of a flight in the back seat of a fast jet must be right up there with a substantial win on the National Lottery. For Bob Cossey, membership secretary of the 74 Squadron Association, this dream came true in 1989 when he was invited to fly in F-4J Phantom ZE363 'W' during a sortie over the North Sea from Wattisham. The following account was written shortly after the flight and was first published in the Association Newsletter, *Tiger News*.

"Tiger One, clear roll." Squadron Leader John Sims released the brakes of the Phantom and engaged reheat and we began to move. The big jet surged forward with an ear splitting roar and quickly gathered momentum. Within fifteen seconds we were airborne at the start of a maximum power climb; at 300 knots John cleaned up and we shot skywards sitting on twin columns of thrust that pushed us to 25,000 ft within eighty seconds. Once there we levelled off in a manner not unlike reaching the top of a steep roller coaster ascent when the stomach continues up whilst the body doesn't. We had escaped the grey sheet of cloud which covered RAF Wattisham and the surrounding Suffolk countryside into a world of blue and gold. There could hardly have been a more exhilarating start to any flight and this demonstration of the performance capabilities of an old but still very potent warplane proved that it could still hold its own in the world of modern fly-by-wire fighters.

'The day had begun with an early drive down from Norwich. At Wattisham the first call was to the station surgery for a full medical by the SMO – ears, nose and throat, heart and lungs, blood pressure, eyesight and hearing, and one or two other things as well! I was lectured on the possible effects of 'g' and what to do with the onset of a blackout and tunnel vision if the blood started to pool in the lower parts of the body. Another possible effect of a ride in a high performance aeroplane is one of discomfort caused by the trapping of air pockets in the body; behind fillings in teeth for example. In the event I was glad to find that I wasn't bothered by either problem.

As part of the preparation for the flight a very necessary forty-five minutes was spent going through emergency procedures. Nobody likes to anticipate that such a thing is likely to happen, but by the same token it can, and does, and it is vital that you are ready to meet it with a working knowledge of what to do, or at least with having been told what to do. Exactly what would have been remembered in the event of a serious emergency is difficult to say. So it was that I explored the world of escape procedures, ejection seats, survival techniques and dinghy drills. The sortie was to be flown on a command ejection basis – that is, John would initiate any ejection, bearing in mind that he would know best when enough was enough if anything did go wrong! (command ejection was unique to the F-4J in RAF service; the Phantom FGR.2 did not have it). There was always the possibility that the system could fail and as with all systems on modern military aircraft there are back up procedures. In this case I was told that if the pilot disappeared and I stayed put then obviously something was very wrong and I should initiate my own ejection by pulling the black and yellow striped handle between my legs smartly up to my chin. If that failed there was the handle above my head which should be pulled down over the face. If that failed too then it just wasn't to be my day and I would have to resort to baling out in the time honoured manner – i.e. releasing the canopy, for which there was an emergency handle on the sill, and climbing out!

Assuming the ejection sequence worked as it should, the Martin Baker Mark H7 zero zero seat would punch me well clear of the tailplane and fin, the drogue and then the main parachute would deploy and the seat would fall away. That would leave me time to collect my thoughts as I descended and anticipate the next actions required. If the ejection had been over land, all well and good, all I would have to do would be to cushion the impact on landing by bending my legs and rolling. If over the sea, I would have to jettison the chute just prior to immersion and deploy the dinghy and get into it, which in a choppy sea would be no easy matter. There were, of course, distress beacons and flares as an integral part of the survival kit, as well as rations, a baler – and the knowledge that if all went well an SAR helicopter would be plucking me out of the water within forty-five minutes of ejection!

It was with the possibility of immersion in the cold inhospitable North Sea in mind that my kitting out for the flight took place. As a complete novice I was given plenty of help, but crews normally dressed themselves. It was easier for them anyway in as much as they had their own suits and harnesses on which strapping tension was already predetermined to fit their frames. My problem was that being of rather large build, clothing that actually fitted was not easy to find and in the end it was thanks to several squadron members that a composite suit/harness could be found. First on were the thermal long johns, singlet and thick woollen socks. An ordinary flying suit went over the top of this, as did flying boots. That was the easy bit!

Next came the g-suit which fitted very tightly around the legs and lower abdomen, necessarily so, so that it could do its job of constricting the flow of blood properly, as it inflated when the effects of gravity, or indeed lack of it, were encountered. Over this went the immersion suit itself, tightly fitting around wrists, ankles and neck, and very snug over the rest of the body, as well as being extremely warm as it was made of a rubberised material which trapped an insulating layer of air beneath it. Then the harness which, once in position, felt somewhat like a strait jacket until you got used to the tightness of the strapping. There was a great tendency to walk in a slightly strange manner until you learned not to bend double in an attempt to relieve the constriction of the kit. The bone dome and mask had to be very carefully selected and adjusted to ensure freedom of movement, without being loose in the case of the former, and without the possibility of an oxygen leak in the latter. As a final touch, two little bags were popped into the pockets of the suit 'just in case' – but I was delighted to find that I did not need to use either of them!

The whole kitting out process took over forty-five minutes but, as everything connected with a flight in a high performance aeroplane, it had, by necessity, to be thorough and without compromise. When fully dressed in all the essential gear the Phantom crew member carried an additional 50 lb in weight on his back. When on QRA he wore all this for twenty-four hours at a stretch, with the exception of the harness and helmet, so that he could react with speed to the alarm and not waste precious seconds having to dress. The kit that 74 Squadron crews wore on the F-4J was all American and differed considerably from the RAF equivalent – for example the harnessing was an integral part of the seat in RAF configured aircraft which the crew member strapped into once he had taken up his position in the cockpit. So there I was: medical completed, emergency procedures hopefully firmly in my mind, flying kit on – now for the briefing.

No. 74 Squadron was a small unit by RAF standards with just fourteen aeroplanes and consequently they were always very busy in their effort to meet their flying task each month. On this particular day they had F-4Js down at Cambrai working with the French Air Force Tiger Squadron, F-4Js up at Coningsby doing Air Combat Training with Tornado F.3s of 229 OCU and, apart from those in the Aircraft Servicing Flight (ASF) or in deep maintenance at St Athan, the remainder were engaged in a gunnery validation exercise testing some new Ferranti software in conjunction with target towing Canberras from 100 Squadron at RAF Wyton. That left literally just one aircraft available for my flight. Initially the plan was for us to participate in one of the gunnery sorties, flying as a radar sweep for another Phantom (flown by C.O. Wing Commander Cliff Spink) which would do the actual firing. We would then spend some time exploring a small part of the Phantom's capabilities away from the gunnery area before returning to Wattisham. That plan was amended when, after some unserviceability developed in the trials aircraft, I was given the option of waiting until the problem had been resolved, or going solo on a sortie exploring a larger part of the flight envelope of the F-4J. A pairs sortie would undoubtedly have been brilliant, with the attendant possibilities for air-to-air photography, but the alternative option won the day.

Once I was ready for the briefing, John Sims led the way into the Ops Room within the hardened operational block and in a twenty minute session we covered in detail exactly what we were going to do once airborne. There was the weather, fuel states and diversions to consider too. On this particular day a continuous cloud sheet covered East Anglia as a whole and stretched out over the North Sea where we would be operating for the duration of the flight. Its base was between 2,500 and 3,000 feet but it was only a few hundred feet thick and it would take only a matter of seconds to break through into clear blue after take-off. Above that there would be nothing to worry us and with it being a slow moving weather pattern, Met were happy that there would be no changes apart from the possibility of an odd shower as we returned to base. Nevertheless, operations were always flown with two possible diversions. Our weather diversion was to be Manston in Kent. Weather diversions are usually a fair distance away from home base so that if the weather should change dramatically, despite assurances that it won't, there is a very good chance that the diversion isn't similarly affected. If we did have to use Manston, we would transit there at low level to avoid all the Airways traffic going into London's airports. The crash diversion was to be Honington – a rather dramatic term for a short range diversion which would be used in the event of the runway at Wattisham being blocked by another aircraft (or vehicle) at the last moment.

As far as recovery to Wattisham itself was concerned, the Duty Officer (Flying) positioned in the tower would decide what form this should take. Because of the risk of showers he had decided on radar recovery, which meant that we would be obliged to contact base prior to recovery, tell them who we were, where we were and what we wanted to do. They would then give us a radar approach until we became visual, after which we could opt to fly straight in and land or, as we did eventually do, complete a few circuits. It so happened that ATC were looking for controller training themselves and they requested a GCA in which poor weather would be simulated and we would be talked all the way in. As far as fuel was concerned there was a restriction of 3,500 lb remaining on the ground, this reserve being necessary to get us comfortably to the crash diversion. The reserve is chosen with the range of the diversion airfield in mind (and the likely weather) and although 3,500 lb sounded to be a little on the high side, especially for an airfield relatively close to Wattisham, John explained they too might be subject to showers and an instrument approach might have to be made, requiring more fuel.

John then briefed me as to the procedure he would adopt in case of an emergency, bearing in mind I had already had detailed instructions on this. Essentially, it was made clear that he would initiate any ejection. Most importantly from my point of view, he would keep me fully informed of any problems which might crop up. To him a problem might be a minor one but because of radio exchanges between him and the ground I might start to get the idea that some dramatic situation was developing, whereas in fact it might be far less serious than I was imagining. In the event the flight went without any hitch at all and the 'J' behaved impeccably, however, I did have trouble with the intercom and for much of the sortie was unable to hear clearly what was being said to me and to the ground.

Briefing complete, and after a 'nervous wee' (not an easy matter with all that gear on) we walked out to Hardened Aircraft Shelter (HAS) 30 where F-4J ZE363 'W' sat waiting for us, ground crew busily fussing around her. I climbed straight up to the navigator's position and Flying Officer 'Spikey' Whitmore set about strapping me in, connecting all the necessary pipes and cables and removing the seat pins and stowing them beside me. I could thereby see that my seat was now live. While this was going on, John went into the HAS management cabin and signed for the aeroplane, having looked at the paperwork and noted any limitations relating to it. It may have been, for example, that a particular system was not working properly and therefore must not be used. Alternatively, modifications may have been done which John had to be aware of; he also needed to satisfy himself that all essential maintenance had been completed and that the aircraft had been fuelled. In our case we had 17,500 lb on board. He then did a walk round, checking the aircraft externally, satisfying himself that everything was as it should be. My own pre-take-off routine centred on familiarising myself with the instruments which I would be watching throughout the sortie – altimeter, mach meter and artificial horizon in particular – and receiving instruction on the canopy locking mechanism and the checks necessary to ensure that it was properly closed.

This done, and with John by now in the front seat, the oxygen mask with its integral microphone was switched on and the regulator adjusted. It took a little while to get used to breathing through the mask but, as with everything else, I found that I quickly adapted to it and within a few minutes my breathing became almost normal with reduced tendency to gasp and over-ventilate. It was the same with the cockpit environment as a whole which was far more comfortable than I had anticipated. Ergonomically the Phantom was no match for the new breed of fighters, but it was not as restrictive in room or visibility, given all the kit I was wearing and the relatively high sills of the rear cockpit, as might have been expected. Forward visibility was somewhat hampered by the pilot's seat, but by peering down either side I could see beyond it. The other difficult area was over the shoulder where my own seat, the fuselage and the relative difficulty of turning my head beyond 90 degrees all conspired against me.

Once it had been established that I was comfortable and feeling OK, John did his 'left to right' cockpit checks and then contacted Squadron Ops and the Ground Control for permission to start engines. The doors at the rear of the HAS were opened and the engines were spooled up in sequence. There were no engine instruments in the rear cockpit so I was unable to watch the process, although John talked me through it – as he did the whole sortie. The F-4J required an air start, a system which was not necessary in the British Phantom FGR.2 which had internal start. John signalled to the ground crew by putting a fist into the palm of his hand and they powered up the air from the external generators to the aircraft. He then gave the No. 2 (right) engine start-up signal (a finger in the air moved in a circular motion above the head) and flicked the toggle switch from left to right which allowed air in against the turbine blades of the engine and which blew it up to about 10 per cent rpm. As it hit this figure, John opened the throttle and pressed the relight button to activate high tension igniters which could be heard making a 'cracking' noise, and after a couple of seconds ignition occurred. Once alight, Exhaust Gas Temperatures (EGTs) started to rise. These were watched closely to make sure they did not exceed 700°C. As rpm and airflow increased, the temperatures started to drop back (it was only when the engine was turning slowly with a high fuel flow during the start-up procedure that temperatures had really climbed).

Once the engine was turning, rpm wound up quite quickly and on passing 45 per cent the starter was cut off. At 65 per cent John checked that the EGT and the nozzles had stabilised and that the associated hydraulic and oil pressures were as they should be. Oil controlled gearboxes and nozzles were particularly important, as was the constant speed drive unit from the gearbox to the internal generator. The latter could not be switched on before oil pressure was below 50 lb/sq.in, otherwise seals would blow. Once done, the whole procedure was repeated for the left (No. 1) engine.

With both General Electric J79s alight and running, John taxied Whisky forward out of the HAS on to the hard stand in front. Even with the canopy still up there was surprisingly little awareness of engine noise, largely because of the insulation of the helmets. The ground crew now assisted with the functional tests, the flaps, aileron, rudder and air brakes were all exercised so that it could be confirmed that they were working properly and that the hydraulic rams which operated them were not leaking. Ground crew also checked that air was blowing across the leading and trailing edge flaps to confirm that the boundary layer control was functioning correctly. The hook was cycled and seen to be working before being stowed away. The final check was of the auto-stabilisation system. Once ground crew and pilot were happy we were given permission to proceed to Runway 05. Up front John continued with his checks as we taxied and all the while there was chatter on the radio, not all directed at us, but between the tower and other aircraft, all of which was listened to as it gave a very good idea of the activity around the airfield and enabled a mental picture to be built up of the local air traffic environment. Then at last we were on the threshold with John holding the Phantom on the brakes while running the engines up to 85 per cent power. It was at that moment that my adrenaline really started to flow!

Inevitably, I had preconceived ideas about what a flight in an F-4 would be like – but the reality was a thousand times better! The punch in the back as the brakes were released and reheat engaged was the first of many indications I was to have over the course of the next hour as to the power and capability of the then thirty-year-old, but still extremely potent, design. ZE363 surged forward and at 145 knots, fifteen seconds after brake release, John rotated and we cleaned up and climbed away in spectacular fashion in a maximum performance climb to 25,000 ft. The angle of climb was acute, speed increasing all the while, and it was barely eighty seconds later that we levelled out. Normally reheat would have been cancelled at 300 knots at 500–600 ft followed by a cruise climb in cold power to the transit level of 15,000 ft to save fuel. But on this occasion, and throughout the sortie, John was out to show me exactly what the Phantom was capable of. So he descended again to 3,500 ft and we did a climb back to 25,000 ft without reheat to demonstrate the contrast. This really was a more sedate and gentlemanly way of doing things and there was a very noticeable difference in the angle of attack. This was not surprising as in reheat the engines were developing 35,640 lb of thrust between them but in cold power this figure was reduced to just 23,600 lb.

Once at 25,000 ft for the second time we began to accelerate. John couldn't get the Wattisham TACAN to work and so had to use others to get a range and bearing so that he could work out our position. We coasted out near Blakeney on the North Norfolk coast and flew twenty miles beyond over the sea before turning almost directly east for a supersonic run (at this distance you avoid dropping a sonic boom across land). Having established our new heading, John accelerated and, even more so at 25,000 ft, you could feel the power coming on as the burners lit. However, the actual transition to supersonic speed was a singularly undramatic affair. There was no sensation within the aircraft itself. The instruments registered the transonic jump and the altimeter fluctuated for a brief second – but that was all. Just numbers on a dial. To those who cross the barrier as a regular part of their daily routine that may be the case, but to me it was a milestone in my flying experience! Once we were supersonic it was noticeable that the acceleration thereafter was relatively poor. This was entirely due to the gun pack which was hanging from the fuselage. Although it was streamlined, the front of it was open, a gaping hole from which the muzzle protruded. Once supersonic the shock waves attached themselves to it and drag was created – not conducive to fast acceleration. Between M1.2 and M1.3 we experienced slight vibration and John decelerated, explaining as he did so that the gun was not a preferred weapon because of the limitations we had just encountered. Missiles were normally carried, but the fact remained that the gun pod was still a valid option, particularly in an electronic environment where it may have been impossible to use missiles, or where an adversary was throwing out flares to decoy them. Of course as a straight line weapon a gun was useful in that it could not be electronically jammed or disrupted.

The restrictions of the pod were demonstrated again a little later when we were vectored on to a high flying target by Neatishead radar which was just twenty miles away. John engaged burners but we were 10,000 ft below the target which was at 30,000 ft and we struggled to get to his height at speed, simply because of the gun pack. After the supersonic run we had descended to 15,000 ft and started asking for 'trade'. Before the briefing John had telephoned Neatishead asking them for an area in which to 'play' but at that stage, they were unable to confirm where that area would be. Once we were in situ he arbitrarily chose one off the Lincolnshire and Norfolk coasts, a favourite area in which there were normally a lot of potential targets, both RAF and USAF. His choice was a good one and radar did us proud.

We had three interceptions in fifteen minutes and with the first one came my first experience of pulling 'g'. We were vectored onto a Tornado F.3 from Coningsby and John immediately got a visual on it. Without hesitation he snapped Whisky into a tight turn and almost immediately the suit I was wearing inflated around my lower abdomen and legs. We were exceeding 4 g. I tried to move but an almost intolerable weight was pushing me into the seat. I had a pen in my hand with which I had been writing notes on my knee pad and it snapped in my fingers! "Can you see him? Can you see him?" John's voice was echoing in my helmet. See him? How the hell could I see him when my head was firmly fixed in the position it was when he had suddenly thrown the F-4J into this unnatural (for me) situation. Then, just as suddenly as it had begun, the turn ceased and I could move again. I scanned the clear blue outside for a sight of our adversary, but to no avail. John was still trying to put us into the best position for a simulated missile attack, however, the Tornado was aware of us and was adopting tactics which made it very difficult for us to gain an advantage.

This was exactly where the benefits of these intercepts came in as it gave both parties, the offensive and the defensive, the chance to practice evasive and attacking tactics. Even for the most experienced of pilots, practise interceptions (PIs) were invaluable and essential ongoing training and carried out on an almost daily basis. All are completed within certain rules in the interest of safety but restrictions do not tend to detract from the tactical value of each sortie. There are no limitations as far as the aeroplane itself is concerned other than regard for its maximum 'g' and maximum speed. But if under GCI control there are, for example, minimum ranges to which a target can be approached without visual or radar contact; there are also minimum break-off ranges once the interception is underway, or a height stagger is introduced so that the attacking aircraft will miss its adversary in the vertical rather than in the plan view. The essence of fighter control is the bringing of aircraft together, but only in as safe a manner as possible and squadrons operate under strict standing rules.

Normally of course the navigator would have been using his radar to set up attack profiles and to simulate missile firing. Today it was a purely visual affair from our point of view – or rather John's, as I had still not managed to find the Tornado! No worry. Once the interception was over John climbed above our opposition and inverted the Phantom. There he was, right above me. Or was it below? During the course of the sortie I found that I had great difficulty in relating to the aircraft's attitude, particularly when we were well above the cloud layer and there were no external references. It was only by carefully watching the instruments that I was able to glean some idea as to what we were doing in terms of heading and so forth. In fact much of the sortie was flown 'on instruments' as far as I was concerned which, allied with John's constant updating of information, enabled me to keep abreast of the situation – for some of the time at least!

Our second target was a 56 Squadron Phantom, 74's sister squadron at Wattisham at the time. Neatishead put us on to him and immediately we were turning tightly in an attempt to gain an advantage. By now I was getting used to these high 'g' turns and whilst still finding movement very restrictive, was listening for the call which would warn me we were about to enter the chase, so at least I could be looking outside when the manoeuvring started. As John explained during the debrief after we landed, there was a delay between first identifying potential targets and being given permission to go for them because our controller was co-ordinating with the agency that was controlling the opposition. For instance, if London was controlling an aircraft and they could see another unidentified target echo which was doing everything possible to head for their own, they would be liable to get pretty cross about it, as well as getting pretty worried too (this neatly sums up the difference between air traffic and fighter control, the former existing to keep aircraft apart, the latter to bring them closer together!) So their permission, and the permission of the crew, had to be sought before the interception could be initiated. On one occasion we had the chance of a pair of F-16s from the Continent but were pulled away when that permission was not forthcoming. They were at 35,000 ft and we were heading east at the time but at twenty-five miles we were told that they were in transit to a UK air base and were not available.

I was having as much trouble getting a visual on the Firebird's Phantom as I had been with the Tornado. As with learning to cope with the effects of 'g' and being able to fly and operate the aircraft's systems under those circumstances (I was later told that navigators, when using their radar, tended to lay their head on the scope when 'g' became excessive to help relieve the forces), crews were also taught how to pick out aircraft at considerable distances against the backcloth of a bright blue sky. It was simply a function of experience and practise, and evolved around learning to use the eyes properly. Normally when flying in clear weather you don't consciously focus your eyes on anything. They do in fact focus three or four feet beyond the canopy and, although you might think you are looking beyond that, you are not. So when you are looking for something that you don't know the range of, it follows that you don't know where to focus your eyes. You may be looking directly at the target but because your eyes are not focused properly, it disappears into the background. The trick therefore is to judge the sort of focal length you want for your eyes. The RAF trains its crews to look at something like a cloud, or the aircraft's wingtip to give them horizon and range reference. Thus John was picking things up straight away, whereas I was having the greatest difficulty in locating our targets.

I did eventually manage to pick up the other Phantom thanks to a piece of kit in the rear cockpit of the F-4J. This was a sight which was used for the visual identification of targets and it allowed me to see the other aircraft when we were in the right position. It was known as the TESS (Telescopic Sighting System) and was a British adaptation of a US Marine Corps idea. Acting on the same principle as a periscope, the external lens was mounted just outside the cockpit and the instrument was bore sighted to the aircraft so that when the pilot acquired the target in his sight, the target was also visible to him through the TESS. The British adaptation brought it into the back cockpit for the navigator's use. The whole idea was to get as early an identification as possible and TESS aimed to preclude the need to get too close to a target for visual identification on the basis that it might be hostile. At night different techniques had to be used – such as moving in as close as radar would allow and resorting to the mark one eyeball!

Our third practise interception was on the Canberra TT.18 with which 74 Squadron were working on the gunnery evaluation described earlier. It was *en route* to the firing range. A little later the Boss (Cliff Spink) offered himself as a target as he climbed out of Wattisham but by that time we were watching our fuel state and, as there were still a couple of items on the agenda which John wished to complete before recovery, we politely declined the offer. Instead we descended to 3,500 ft, immediately above the cloud sheet for a low level acceleration. Of all the things that we did in Whisky that day this was to remain as my most vivid memory. Reducing speed to 300 knots as we skimmed over the cloud tops, John then pushed the throttle through the gate. The power was phenomenal. I was pushed back into my seat as we surged forward at an indescribable rate with a white blur of cloud vapour flashing past the canopy. The whole thing was magnificently exciting! We accelerated to 550 knots and then, to avoid going supersonic as we sped towards the Suffolk coast, John had to pull us into a vertical climb, cancel the reheat and throttle back to bleed off the speed as quickly as possible. It was the ram effect which helped facilitate such tremendous acceleration and 74 Squadron's crews were unanimous in their praise of the J79 engines of the F-4J for their immediate response to throttle. The turbofan Spey Phantoms may have had a better take-off performance, but once in the air the General Electric turbojets performed more efficiently.

Having pulled Whisky into the climb John then took the opportunity to aerobat the Phantom for a few minutes, flying barrel rolls and Derry turns, but not looping it because of the considerable constraints of the gun pod which would have made the manoeuvre a little sluggish over the top. Then he was calling Wattisham for a radar recovery. We made a good GCA with little deviation from the line, in either height or angle, and came in for a roller, climbing away again to do one visual circuit – all that our remaining fuel allowed – before touching down again, deploying the drogue and braking cautiously due to the absence of any anti-skid braking system on the F-4J. As our speed slowed we raised our canopies and exited the runway, keeping masks in place so that John and I could continue to converse as he explained the end of flight checks that were started as we were still taxiing. We had been airborne for sixty-five minutes and during that time we had burned 14,000 lb of fuel – something over six tons!

As we re-entered 74 Squadron's HAS complex there was a small party of visiting VIPs interestedly watching and I certainly felt like a king! We stopped outside HAS 30 and John shut the engines down. The tug arrived, the tow bar was fitted and we were reversed into the shelter. Then it was mask off, helmet off, stow the pins in the ejector seat, release straps, climb on to the top of the port intake, walk back and slide onto the wing and jump down to ground level. It was only then that I realised how tired I felt. I was a little breathless too, taking time to readjust to breathing without a mask, but the short walk back to the crew room and a good strong cup of coffee helped me to relax. The adrenaline had started to flow a little less quickly by this stage too and by the time that we got back to the Ops Room for the debrief I was well and truly back on terra firma. De-kitting was a faster process than kitting up and it was some relief to remove the warm constraints of the clothing. By the time that I was due to leave the squadron Cliff Spink had returned from his trip. He nudged John in the ribs and said "I wonder how long it will take for that smile to be wiped off his face?" Well, it's over sixteen years since that flight and I am still smiling broadly, even more so after a low-level sortie through the mountains of Wales in a Hawk from RAF Valley, but that, as they say, is another story!

Glossary

AAA	Anti-Aircraft Artillery
A&AEE	Aeroplane and Armament Experimental Establishment
AADRS	Automatic Aileron Droop Retraction System
AAM	Air-to-air missile
ACM	Air Combat Manoeuvring
ADI	Attitude Director Indicator
AEW	Airborne Early Warning
AFB	Air Force Base
AFCS	Automatic Flight Control System
AGL	Above Ground Level
AIM	Air Intercept Missile
AOA	Angle of Attack
AOG	Aircraft On Ground
APCS	Automatic Power Compensation System
ASF	Aircraft Servicing Flight
ATAF	Allied Tactical Air Force
ATC	Air Traffic Control
AUW	All-up Weight
BAe	British Aerospace
BINGO fuel	Minimum fuel warning
BLC	Boundary Layer Control
CAP	Combat Air Patrol
CG	Centre of Gravity
CMRP	Continuous Mosaic Radar Prediction
CRT	Cathode Ray Tube
CSDU	Constant Speed Drive Unit
CTTO	Central Tactics and Trials Organisation
EAS	Equivalent Airspeed
ECM	Electronic Countermeasures
EGT	Exhaust Gas Temperature
ERU	Ejector Release Unit

FAA	Fleet Air Arm
GCA	Ground Controlled Approach
GCI	Ground Controlled Interception
GTS	Gas Turbine Starter
HAS	Hardened Aircraft Shelter
HF	High Frequency
HSA	Hawker Siddeley Aviation
HSI	Horizontal Situation Indicator
IAS	Indicated Airspeed
IF	Instrument Flying
IFF	Identification Friend or Foe
IMC	Instrument Meteorological Conditions
IMN	Indicated Mach Number
INAS	Inertial Navigation and Attack System
ISA	International Standard Atmosphere
JPT	Jet Pipe Temperature
KCAS	Knots Calibrated Airspeed
LRU	Line Replaceable Units
MLS	Minimum Launch Speed
MTBF	Mean Time Between Failures
MTBR	Mean Time Between Rejection
NATC	Naval Air Test Center
NATO	North Atlantic Treaty Organisation
NATOPS	Naval Air Training and Operating Procedures Standardization Programme
NCO	Non-commissioned Officer
OCU	Operational Conversion Unit
PAN call	Radio transmission concerning aircraft safety
PD	Pulse Doppler
PI	Practise Interception
PIO	Pilot Induced Oscillation
PWR	Passive Warning Receiver
QFI	Qualified Flying Instructor
QRA	Quick Reaction Alert
RAT	Ram Air Turbine
RHAG	Rotary Hydraulic Arrester Gear
RIO	Radar Intercept Officer
RP	Rocket Projectile
SACLANT	Supreme Allied Commander Atlantic
SACEUR	Supreme Allied Commander Europe
SAM	Surface to Air Missile
SAR	Search and Rescue

SFI	Special Flying Instruction
SMO	Senior Medical Officer
SNCO	Senior Non-commissioned Officer
SNEB	A type of 68 mm unguided pod-launched rocket
TACAN	Tactical Air Navigation System
TACEVAL	Tactical Evaluation
TBO	Time Between Overhaul
TESS	Telescopic Sighting System
UCM	Uncommanded Control Movement
UHF	Ultra High Frequency
USAF	United States Air Force
USMC	United States Marine Corps
VHF	Very High Frequency
WSO	Weapon System Operator
WST	Weapon System Trainer

Appendix One

Phantom FGR.2 Performance and Speed Limitations

MAX REHEAT TAKE-OFF ACCELERATION AND CLIMB

DRAG INDEX 15 – AUW 45,000 lb

Altitude (ft)	Fuel (lb)	Time (mins)	Distance (nm)
To climb speed 400 kts/0.85 M	1,600	0.5	1.5
20,000	2,370	1.1	7
30,000	2,730	1.5	11
35,000	**2,920**	**1.9**	**14**
40,000	3110	2.4	18

DRAG INDEX 40 – AUW 55,000 lb

Altitude (ft)	Fuel (lb)	Time (mins)	Distance (nm)
To climb speed 350 kts/0.82 M	1,800	0.6	2
20,000	2,860	1.4	9
30,000	**3,400**	**2.1**	**15**
40,000	4,100	3.4	26

Note 1 – Fuel figures are from start-up. An allowance of 500 lb is included for taxiing and engine run-ups.
Note 2 – Time and distance figures are from wheels rolling.
Note 3 – Optimum cruise altitude figures are in bold type.

MAX REHEAT TAKE-OFF TO 300 KCAS, THEN MIL POWER

DRAG INDEX 15 – AUW 45,000 lb

Altitude (ft)	Fuel (lb)	Time (mins)	Distance (nm)
To climb speed 400 kts/0.85 M	1,400	1.0	3.5
20,000	2,100	3.8	24
30,000	2,450	6.4	43
35,000	**2,700**	**8.5**	**60**

DRAG INDEX 35 – AUW 55,000 lb

Altitude (ft)	Fuel (lb)	Time (mins)	Distance (nm)
To climb speed 350 kts/0.82 M	1,450	1.1	4
20,000	2,500	5.3	39
25,000	2,850	7.3	48
30,000	**3,250**	**10.5**	**74**

SELECTED SPEED/G LIMITATIONS

	Max Speed		Max G	
Configuration	KCAS	Mach No.	Normal	Rolling
Wing tanks – Empty	750	1.6	−2 to +5	0 to +3.8
Wing tanks – Under 75 per cent full	550	1.6	−2 to +4	0 to +3.5
Wing tanks – Over 75 per cent full	550	1.6	−1 to +3.5	0 to +1.5

Configuration	Max Speed		Max G	
	KCAS	Mach No.	Normal	Rolling
CL tank – full	600	1.8	0 to +2.5	1 only
CL tank – under 75 per cent full	600	1.8	0 to +4	1 to +2.5
Probe – moving	300	0.9	–	–
Probe – extended	400	0.9	–	–
Gear/flaps ext	250	–	–	–
RAT out	515	1.1	Moving 0 to +2.5 Extended −1 to +4	
Chute deploy	200	–	–	–

Minimum speeds

15 to 30,000 ft – 150 knots
30 to 45,000 ft – 170 knots
45 to 60,000 ft – 200 knots

APPENDIX TWO

Phantom FGR.2 Selected Emergency Procedures

ENGINE FAILURES

SINGLE ENGINE FAILURE DURING TAKE-OFF

TAKE-OFF ABANDONED (AT OR BELOW V-STOP)

Throttle	IDLE
DRAG CHUTE	Stream
Wheel brakes	Apply as required
Hook	Down

Subsequent action – if aborting for other reasons, shut down one engine (right engine if practicable).

TAKE-OFF CONTINUED (ABOVE V-STOP)

Good engine	Max reheat
External stores	Jettison after take-off if necessary
Landing gear	UP
Flaps	UP
Affected engine	Throttle OFF (after take-off)

ENGINE FAILURE IMMEDIATELY AFTER TAKE-OFF

Good engine	Max reheat
External stores	Jettison if necessary
Landing gear	UP
Flaps	UP at safe speed
Affected engine	Throttle OFF

MECHANICAL FAILURE

Good engine	Power as required
Throttle of affected engine	OFF
RAT	Extend

Do not attempt to relight.

Non-Mechanical Failure

Good engine	Power as required

Attempt immediate relight with throttle at IDLE.

If no relight:

Throttle of affected engine	OFF
RAT	Extend

Carry out full relight drill.
If unsuccessful – land as soon as possible.

DOUBLE ENGINE FLAME-OUT

RAT	Extend

Attempt immediate relight on one engine with throttle at IDLE – Note: If necessary there is sufficient electrical power available from either the battery or the RAT for a simultaneous double engine relight.

If no relight:

Both throttles	OFF

Establish 250 to 300 KCAS if possible. Carry out **Full Relight Drill** on one engine. Repeat as necessary. If unsuccessful, do not attempt to relight second engine until below 25,000 ft. If engine lights, but fails to accelerate, increase speed within relight envelope. If no acceleration within 1 minute – Throttle OFF. As a last resort, the L ENGINE START switch may be used, below 10,000 ft and 240 knots, to start the left engine via the GT starter (Note – The aux air doors must be open). If no relight – EJECT.

RELIGHTING

IMMEDIATE RELIGHT

Throttle of affected engine	IDLE
Relight button	Press

If no relight within 20 seconds, carry out **Full Relight Drill**. Monitor TGT closely. Attempts to relight outside relight envelope could lead to serious engine over-temperature.

FULL RELIGHT DRILL

The following speed/heights fall within the relight envelopes.

Speed	0.7 M (Avcat) 0.65 M (Avtur/Avtag)
Altitude (maximum)	35,000 ft (Avtur/Avtag) 27,500 ft (Avcat)

Optimum relights are obtained below 25,000 ft; windmilling HP rpm 15 to 18 per cent. **Warning** – Below 10 per cent HP rpm a relight is unlikely and turbine damage may result.

Actions.

Throttle of affected engine	OFF
RAT	Extend

Allow engine to windmill for 2 minutes.

Relight button	Press
Throttle of affected engine	IDLE
TGT and rpm	Monitor – release relight button when TGT rises and rpm reaches 40 per cent minimum

If no rise within 20 seconds or if the engine TGT rapidly approaches 630°C and appears likely to exceed it, or if TGT rises without a corresponding rise in HP rpm, or if the engine fails to accelerate to flight idle within 1 minute:

Throttle of affected engine	OFF

Wait 2 minutes and attempt further relight at lower altitude.

If all relight attempts are unsuccessful:

Throttle of affected engine	OFF

Land as soon as possible.

FIRE/OVHT/ENG WARNINGS

FIRE/OVHT/ENG caption on the ground

Warn navigator.

Throttles	OFF
Engine Master switches	OFF
Brakes	OFF

Evacuate aircraft.

FIRE/OVHT/ENG caption during take-off

Warn navigator.

At or below V-stop

Abandon take-off. Affected engine – Throttle OFF.

When stopped:

Good engine	Throttle OFF
Engine Master switches	OFF

Evacuate aircraft.

Above V-stop

Continue take-off.

Good engine	MAX REHEAT
Affected engine	Carry out appropriate drill when safely airborne
External stores	If necessary jettison after take-off

FIRE/OVHT/ENG caption during flight

Warn navigator.

Good engine	Power as required

If both FIRE and OVHT captions come on or the ENG caption comes on or there are other signs of fire/mechanical failure:

Affected engine	Throttle OFF

Subsequent actions:

RAT	Extend
Affected Engine Master switch	Confirm correct engine, then OFF
ENG BLEED CONTROL -Or- Bleed control switch	Pull ISOLATE

If warning goes out

Operate FIRE TEST. If normal – land as soon as possible using ½ flap.

If warning remains on or FIRE TEST not normal

Look for other signs of fire.

If fire confirmed – EJECT

If fire not confirmed

Land as soon as possible using ½ flap:

If only one FIRE or OVHT caption illuminated and no other symptoms.

Affected engine	Throttle to IDLE

If warning goes out within 5 seconds:

Operate FIRE TEST. If normal – Leave affected engine at IDLE. Land as soon as possible using ½ flap.

If warning remains on or FIRE TEST not normal:

Affected engine	Throttle OFF

Subsequent actions:

RAT	Extend
Affected Engine Master switch	Confirm correct engine, then OFF
ENG BLEED CONTROL	Pull
-Or- Bleed control switch	ISOLATE

If warning goes out (after engine shut down):

Operate FIRE TEST. If normal – land as soon as possible using ½ flap.

If warning remains on or FIRE TEST not normal:

Look for other signs of fire.

If fire confirmed – EJECT

If fire not confirmed:

Land as soon as possible using ½ flap.

EJECTION

Normally navigator ejects first if time and circumstances permit. However, in extreme situations, if the pilot decides that immediate ejection is necessary he should eject (without warning the navigator) and the navigator should follow on seeing the front seat leave the aircraft. Simultaneous or near simultaneous ejections should be avoided. If ejection is inevitable at speeds above 500 KCAS/0.8 M the pilot should eject first. Post-mod 427, either crew member may eject first and/or either canopy may be jettisoned first.

SEAT MINIMA

Ground level, zero speed, no sink rate. If a sink rate exists, minimum ejection altitude is increased by 10 per cent of rate of descent, with 0 degrees bank.

PROCEDURE

Alert navigator. Assume correct ejection position. Pull face screen or seat pan firing handle to full extent.

EJECTION AT HIGH SPEED (PRE-MOD 427)

Reduce speed to below 500 KCAS/0.8 M. If impossible, the front crew member should eject first, otherwise the resultant pressure on the front canopy could prevent separation and render ejection impossible.

IF CANOPY FAILS TO JETTISON

Retain whichever firing handle operated with right hand then: Pull canopy PULL TO JETT handle fully aft.

IF CANOPY STILL FAILS TO JETTISON

Move canopy control lever to OPEN. Pull canopy PULL TO UNLOCK handle fully aft.

WHEN CANOPY SEPARATES

Pull either ejection seat firing handle to full extent.

AUTOMATIC SEPARATION FAILURE

If parachute fails to open at 10,000 ft or after 2 seconds when ejection is below 10,000 ft. Pull emergency harness release handle fully aft. Push free of seat. Locate and pull parachute D-ring to full extent.

MANUAL BALE OUT

Jettison canopies, front first (post-mod 427 either canopy may be jettisoned first).
Operate emergency harness release handle.
Pull off PEC.
Hoist parachute onto shoulder.
If possible, trim nose-down and invert aircraft.
When clear pull rip-cord D-ring. The shoulder riser may have to be pulled down to reach the D-ring which can then be pulled against the grip of the left hand on the riser.

AIRSPEED INDICATOR FAILURE

Flight Condition	Angle of Attack Units
Climb	5.5
Cruise/Endurance	8
Gear extension (flaps up)	9
Flap extension (gear down)	13
On speed +30	13

HYDRAULICS

WARNING 1 – The loss of any hydraulic pump puts on the CHECK HYD GAUGES caption. Any subsequent loss shows only on the respective hydraulic gauge, unless it is a utility pump.

WARNING 2 – Do not taxi with any hydraulic failure, shut down as soon as possible.

SINGLE UTILITY PUMP FAILURE

Land as soon as practicable.
Monitor utility and PC hydraulic pressure gauges.
Be prepared to use overrun cable.

COMPLETE UTILITY SYSTEM FAILURE

Restrict speed to below 0.85 M and 400 KCAS.
Blow down landing gear before pneumatic pressure falls below 2,300 PSI (when range is not critical).
Blow down flaps when required for landing.
AUX AIR DOORS switch – EMERG OPEN.
ANTI-SKID switch – OFF.
Land as soon as practicable (approach-end engagement if possible).

Note 1 – If a complete utility system failure occurs after the flaps are down, still use pneumatic flap lowering.

Note 2 – After a complete utility system failure the following services are inoperative:

Air refuelling probe (normal operation)	Radar antenna drive
Anti-skid	Ramps
ARI	Rudder power control system
Aux air doors (normal operation)	Speed brakes
Arrester hook (retraction)	Stab augs – roll and yaw
Flaps (normal)	Utility powered ailerons and spoilers
Hydraulic fuel transfer pumps	Variable bypass valve
Landing gear (normal operation)	Wheelbrakes (normal operation)
Nose wheel steering	Wing fold (Blocks 31 to 34 only)
Pneumatic air compressor	

COMPLETE UTILITY SYSTEM FAILURE WITH SINGLE PC FAILURE

Reduce speed to below 300 KCAS but not below 230 KCAS with landing gear up.
Jettison any asymmetric load.
If possible fly to an airfield with approach-end cable.
Reduce weight to 36,000 lb or less.

Blow down landing gear at 5,000 ft minimum AGL, if practicable before pneumatic pressure falls below 2,300 psi.

AUX AIR DOORS switch	EMERG OPEN
ANTI-SKID switch	OFF

Land as soon as possible.

Use of flaps.
Cable available – Do not lower flaps.
Cable not available – Blow down flaps at 250 KCAS or below, and at 5,000 ft. Anticipate some loss of lateral control until flaps extended (manual rudder control is available). Carry out a slow-speed handling check but do not get slower than 17 units AOA. As far as possible make all turns into operating wing. Make an approach-end engagement, if possible landing on the runway with least crosswind.

On final approach proceed as follows.
Make a long 17 units AOA approach concentrating on early line up
Full lateral stick may be needed for adequate control.
Fly the 17 units AOA until flaring to 19.2 units AOA for touchdown
Do not get slower than 17 units AOA prior to the flare.
Do not overshoot after touchdown. If the approach-end cable is missed, engage the next arresting system.

ARRESTING CABLE SPEED/AUW LIMITATIONS

PRE-MEDITATED ENGAGEMENT

Weight	Less than 36,000 lb
Without use of brakes	Not more than 5,100 lb in tanks 1 to 6
With use of brakes	Not more than 4,000 lb in tanks 1 to 6
7 tank	Empty or full (not partially full)
Internal and external wing tanks	Empty

EMERGENCY ENGAGEMENT

All-up Weight	RHAG Mk.1
36,000 lb	160 knots
46,000 lb	155 knots
55,000 lb	146 knots
58,000 lb	144 knots

Individual cable maximum speed regardless of weight – 160 knots.

Caution – There is a possibility of internal fuel tanks damage if arresting gears are engaged at high speed and high fuel load.

Index

Aberporth 125
Akrotiri 120, 126–7, 130
Alconbury 100,126
Aldergrove 35
Alkali missile 71
Allison, W/C Denis 103
Allison, S/L John 106–7
Atoll missile 71–2
Avro Shackleton 108, 132

BAe Nimrod 110, 130
Batt, 'Gordie' 111
Beck, W/C Keith 107, 109–110
Bedford 134–5
Bell, F/O Mike 111
Bendell, S/L Anthony 'Bugs' 38–41, 120–1
Blakeney 148
Boscombe Down 34, 123
Botham, F/L John 126
Brough 132
Bruggen 54, 102, 111
Burn, Lt Cdr 13
Burns, 'Bobby' 132

Central Tactics and Trials Organisation (CTTO) 54, 63
Cherry Point 36
Clarke, G/C Graham 129–131
Cohu, W/C Jerry 105
Coningsby 8, 33, 38, 54, 89, 92, 94, 105, 112, 124, 129, 132, 137, 149
Continuous Mosaic Radar Prediction 58
Cossey, Bob 141–153
Curtiss, G/C John 102

Davis, F/L Sandy 109
Davis Monthan AFB 74
Day, F/L Geoff 127
Decimomannu 138
Desmond, W/C Peter 34–6, 102–4, 105–112, 122
Douglas-Boyd, F/L 'John' 40

Edwards AFB 4–5
Elworthy, W/C Tim 126–7
English Electric Lightning 30, 36–7, 120–1
Evans, AVM D.G. 32
Exercise *Braid* 139
Exercise *Cloudy Chorus* 129
Exercise *Limelight* 44

Fairey Gannet 22, 52
Fallis, F/L Dick 126
Farnborough 20
Fassberg 132
Finningley 112
Flint, Cdr Laurence E. 5
Frick, Heinz 35

Gibb, S/L Graham 104
Gibson, Vice-Admiral D.C.E.F. 18
Grumman TF-9J Cougar 36

Hammill, F/L Jack 10
Handley Page Victor 108, 127
Hawker P.1154 6–7
Hay, Capt Gus 127
Headley, Don 132–140
Hefford, Cdr 13
Hickson, Capt K.R. 30
High Wycombe 54, 124
Hine, W/C Paddy 102
HMS *Ark Royal* 42–53, 101
HMS *Eagle* 8, 12, 42, 62
Hodges, S/L David 105
Holme-on-Spalding Moor 133–6
Honington 144
Hughes, F/L Norman 103

James, F/L Steve 100
Jaybird (MiG-21 radar) 72
Jindivik 125, 130
Jordan, Capt J. B. 6

Karup 90
Keflavik 111
Kennedy, F/L Hugh 105
Kinloss 109
Kirkbymoorside 140
Kirriemuir 110

Lambert Field 4
Larkhill range 35
Leeming 129
Leuchars 8, 25, 53, 63, 105, 107, 109
Little, Robert C. 4
Lockheed F-104 Starfighter 6

MacFadyen, W/C Ian 126
Manston 144
Marshall, Lt Cdr Peter 25
Martin, AM Sir Harold 32
Mayner, F/L Barry 109
McDill AFB 6
McDonnell FH-1 Phantom 1
McDonnell F2H Banshee 1
McDonnell F3H Demon 2
McRobb, F/L Keith 126
MiG-17 23
MiG-19 3
MiG-21 3, 23, 60, 66, 68, 71–2
MiG-23 64, 72
MiG-25 64
Miramar 6
Mountbatten 106

Neatishead 149
North, F/L 138
North American A-5 Vigilante 3
North Luffenham 105
Nottingham, Jim 138

Pack, G/C John 110
Palin, W/C Roger 110
Panavia Tornado F.3 129–130, 149
Patuxent River 5, 9, 28
Pearson, Cdr A. M. G. 18
Pearson, Jack 139
Pizzey, Jack 129
Pollington, F/O David 104
Project *Sageburne* 5
Project *Skyburner* 5
Project *Top Flight* 5

Republic F-105 Thunderchief 38–9
Robertson, F/L Graham 122

Schnabel, Major Jim 107
SEPECAT Jaguar 30, 62, 130
Shaw, G/C Mike 36–8, 94, 100, 119–120
Sims, S/L John 141–153
South Cerney 129
Spink, W/C Cliff 144, 152–3
Spin Scan B (MiG-21 radar) 71
St Louis 7, 28
Stoner, S/L Tom 106
Sukhoi Su-15 64, 72
Sutton, W/C John 102

Tupolev Tu-16 Badger 22, 108
Tupolev Tu-22 Blinder 22
Tupolev Tu-95 Bear 22, 108

Uncommanded Control Movements 88
USS *Coral Sea* 9
USS *Forrestal* 6
USS *J. F. Kennedy* 11

Vine, Arthur 132
Vliehors range 98, 105

Wahn 103
Watling, F/L Pat 100
Wattisham 129, 141–153
Watton 121
West Freugh 123
Wildenrath 54, 129
Winkles, S/L Al 107
Whitehead, Derek 132
White Sands Missile range (New Mexico) 5
Whitmore, F/L 'Spikey' 145
Woodhall Spa 139
Woods, F/L Guy 112–8, 121–9
Wright, F/O Tim 110
Wyton 144

Yak-25 60
Yeovilton 7, 18, 43, 48, 52, 135

RAF Squadrons

6 – 33, 38, 54, 97, 120
14 – 54, 62, 102, 104
17 – 54, 62, 95, 102, 104
29 – 112, 125
31 – 54, 62, 103–5
41 – 33
43 – 8, 25, 53, 63, 105, 107
54 – 33, 54
74 – 74, 130, 141–153
92 – 129
111 – 53, 100
228 OCU – 8, 32, 38, 94, 97

Fleet Air Arm Squadrons

700P – 7, 20, 25
767 – 18, 25
809 – 20
845 – 20
892 – 18, 20

USAF and US Navy Units

12th TFW – 6
56th FIS – 128
525th Aggressor Squadron – 100, 126
VF-74 – 6